writers
and their times

Ray Bradbury and the Cold War

Joseph Kampff and Greg Clinton

Cavendish Square

New York

For Zach
For Soren

Published in 2015 by Cavendish Square Publishing, LLC,
243 5th Avenue, Suite 136, New York, NY 10016

Copyright © 2015 by Cavendish Square Publishing, LLC

First Edition

CPSIA Compliance Information: Batch #WS14CSQ

All websites were available and accurate when this book was sent to press.

Library of Congress Cataloging-in-Publication Data

Kampff, Joseph.
Ray Bradbury and the cold war / Joseph Kampff.
pages cm. — (Writers and their times)
Includes bibliographical references and index.
ISBN 978-1-62712-819-3 (hardcover) ISBN 978-1-62712-821-6 (ebook)
1. Bradbury, Ray, 1920-2012—Criticism and interpretation. 2. Cold War in literature. 3. Cold War—Influence. I. Title.

PS3503.R167Z73 2014
813'.54—dc23

2014006709

Editorial Director: Dean Miller   Designer: Amy Greenan
Editor: Kristen Susienka   Production Manager: Jennifer Ryder-Talbot
Senior Copy Editor: Wendy A. Reynolds   Production Editor: David McNamara
Art Director: Jeffrey Talbot   Photo Research: J8 Media

Printed in the United States of America

writers
and their times

Contents

rightened at all — but peaceful." He glanced in at the girls and th
ng in the bright lamplight, and lowered his voice. "I didn't say any
appened about four nights ago."

"What?"

"A dream I had. I c_____ all going to be over and a voi

Introduction

Historical Perspectives on Possible Worlds

Whether we realize it or not, everybody has a strategy for reading. Meaning never simply coincides with the words on the page, screen, or stone tablet. Texts acquire meanings from their reader's personal experiences and knowledge of the world. When we're younger, our reading strategies tend to be oriented toward what in literary studies is called *reader response*. Reader response criticism is exactly what it sounds like: it examines the way readers respond to literary works to determine their meanings. Reader response criticism might ask if readers find the work funny, sad, or frightening, or ask whether or not they are sympathetic to the **protagonist**.

Around the seventh grade, however, reading strategies shift away from the reader. Instead, strategies revolve around authors as people living and writing during a specific period of time in history, and how the times they lived in influenced their work. In literary studies, this approach to reading that reveals a literary work's meaning in relation to its historical context is called historicism. Historicizing doesn't invalidate your

This fallout shelter sign is still a common sight today, although the threat of a nuclear attack is not a major concern.

personal responses, however. It deepens them.

Three fundamental elements converge to produce a great work of literature: the author as a unique individual, the historical context, and the work's readers. Even timeless works of literature that speak to a wide audience emerge from a particular time and place. While Ray Bradbury's novels and short stories can certainly be appreciated without any knowledge of Bradbury's life, the historical period of the Cold War, or the culture of United States in the mid-twentieth century, your understanding of his works as a reader will be greatly enriched by information about his personal life and historical moment.

Bradbury's works especially lend themselves to reading through the lenses of political and cultural history. He wrote his most important works at the height of the golden age of science fiction (often abbreviated as "SF")—the 1950s and 1960s—just as the Cold War between the West and the Eastern Bloc was escalating. However, while Bradbury himself refers to many of his stories and novels as science fiction, there is another useful term for describing his works: "speculative fiction." Author Margaret Atwood, describing her own relationship to the science fiction genre in *In Other Worlds: SF and the Human Imagination*, draws a distinction between science fiction and speculative fiction:

> What I mean by "science fiction" is those books
> descended from H. G. Wells' *The War of the Worlds*,
> which treats of an invasion by tentacled, blood-sucking
> Martians shot to Earth in metal canisters—things
> that could not possibly happen—whereas, for me,
> "speculative fiction" means plots that descend from Jules
> Verne's books about submarines and balloon travel and
> such—things that really could happen but just hadn't
> completely happened when the authors wrote the books.

As Atwood goes on to point out, however, these genres are
not always so distinct. There is often a bit of SF that slips into
speculative fiction, and vice versa. Bradbury's works straddle the
line between the two.

A historical approach to reading helps clarify these matters.
The basic distinction between speculative fiction and science
fiction is that speculative fiction is possible, while SF isn't. This
raises important questions: At what point in history—and for
whom—are these stories possible or impossible? Today, we can
say with certainty that there are no "tentacled, blood-sucking"
creatures from Mars converging on Earth at this very moment.
But when *The War of the Worlds* aired on the radio as a mock-
news broadcast in 1938, many listeners were scared to death.
In other words, Martians today clearly suggest (impossible)
science fiction. For people of Bradbury's generation, however,
Martians invading Earth appears to have been a definite
possibility. Although, as *The Martian Chronicles* suggests, the
possibility of humans invading Mars may have seemed more
likely to Bradbury himself.

Bradbury's **dystopian** novel *Fahrenheit 451*, on the other
hand, will probably strike many readers today as not simply
(possible) speculative fiction, but as nearly prophetic in some
regards. For example, when Bradbury began to conceive
the novel in the late 1940s, television was just beginning to
supersede radio as the primary form of home entertainment.

Next to today's high-definition large-screen formats (in homes and, in an extreme example, IMAX theaters), early TV screens were decidedly small and primitive. When the novel was published in 1953, its vision of an American household in which giant screens have replaced all four living room walls was merely a future possibility. Today, many Americans are in fact surrounded by screens—really, they're everywhere— and this reality is not far removed from the one imagined in Bradbury's novel. (Far from experiencing our world as the dystopia *Fahrenheit 451* seems to prophesy, however, we tend to enjoy our screens. We can even read books on them!) A basic understanding of the historical moment in which Bradbury wrote *Fahrenheit 451* provides valuable insight into a past that may have looked forward with apprehension to certain aspects of our current world.

In a 1980 interview with his biographer, David Mogen, Bradbury said, "*The Martian Chronicles* and *Fahrenheit 451* come from the same period of my life, when I was warning people. I was preventing futures." Perhaps his most urgent warning was—and still is—against the possible future in which human beings destroy themselves totally. Massive destruction with technologically advanced weapons was certainly on people's minds during the Cold War. It remains a major issue today. Bradbury warned against this possible future explicitly in the final pages of *Fahrenheit 451* when the bombs fell on the city, and "the war began and ended in that instant." However, there's another possible future in which humanity destroys itself that Bradbury's novel warns against. He also warns of a future in which human beings allow themselves to lose the stories, preserved in books and memory, which define them as human in the first place. These stories are histories, and histories are essential for accessing not only our own but others' past, present, and future worlds.

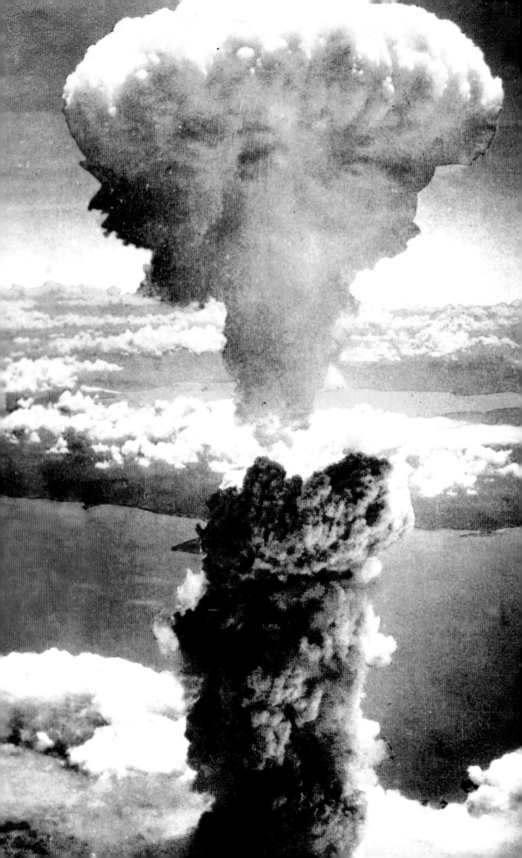

ONE

The Cold War

The Cold War and Literature

Understanding the special anxieties, warnings, and political critiques of Ray Bradbury's fiction requires some knowledge of the Cold War, a period of more than thirty years after World War II that saw the intense rivalry between the United States and the Union of Soviet Socialist Republics, or USSR. The use of nuclear weapons in Japan—the only military deployment of nuclear weapons in history—had a significant impact on the future of politics. The **proxy wars** that were fought in Korea and South Asia caused the deaths of millions of soldiers and civilians, as well as major political turmoil within the U.S. The threat of imminent destruction of humanity represented by the massive nuclear stockpiling that was standard practice by the U.S. and the USSR during the Cold War is also important to understanding Bradbury's works. Space was another frontier in the political conflict, and another source of anxiety as well as promise for Americans during Bradbury's era. McCarthyism gripped the nation for several years, intensifying the sense that the threat to American freedom could come from outside or from inside the United States. Finally, the dissolution of the USSR, which signaled the end of the Cold War, was also a significant influence on Bradbury's work. Each of these aspects of the decades-long tension between the two great superpowers of the twentieth century sheds light on the stories and novels that Bradbury contributed to American literature.

Little Boy and Fat Man

The horrific events that signaled the end of World War II, the bombing of Hiroshima and Nagasaki, remain the only times in history that a nation has used a nuclear weapon in combat. Little Boy, the name of the bomb that was dropped on Hiroshima by the B29 bomber *Enola Gay,* was delivered on August 6, 1945. The explosion killed approximately 80,000 Japanese people, mostly civilians. Approximately 55,000 people died after the bombing from the accumulated effects of burns and radiation sickness. Three days later, on August 9, a bomb named Fat Man was dropped over the Japanese port city of Nagasaki, killing 40,000 people instantly and an additional 10,000 over time. The Japanese signed a declaration of surrender five days later, on August 14, ending the Pacific theater of World War II. The speed and ferocity of the destruction caused by the nuclear bombs shocked the world as it ushered in a new era, one in which Earth-ending weapons were viable for use in armed conflict.

The existence of nuclear weapons added a new dimension of fear and anxiety to foreign diplomacy previously unknown in human history. The United States, Britain, and Canada successfully developed and produced the first nuclear bombs, but they were not the only governments to build a nuclear arsenal. By the 1950s, the worldwide balance of power hinged on the possession of nuclear technology.

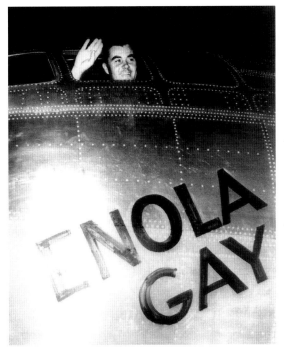

Air Force pilot Colonel Paul W. Tibbets waves out the window before his fateful flight to Japan. On August 6, 1945, he piloted the *Enola Gay* to drop an atomic bomb on Hiroshima, contributing to the end of World War II.

In the period following 1945, nuclear **proliferation**—a quick increase in the number of nuclear bombs created—was in full swing. In 1947, United States President Harry Truman announced a new foreign policy of **containment,** which sought to halt the spread of Communism to other countries by increasing the number of U.S.-supported free-market democracies as well as intervening militarily when Communist forces led revolutions or invasions. Known as the Truman **Doctrine**, this was the first declaration of official tensions between the U.S. and the Soviet Union. The Soviets consolidated power over Eastern Europe, and the U.S. dominated the political sphere of Western Europe. The rest of the world became the stage for proxy wars and political competitions for influence. While the U.S. and the Soviet Union never engaged in any direct armed conflict during the Cold War, the threat of two heavily-armed nuclear powers

11

trading bombs and missiles weighed on the consciousness of many people on the planet.

One feature of the Cold War era that particularly added to the stress of the U.S./Soviet rivalry was the idea of Mutually Assured Destruction, known as MAD. In essence, this state of balanced tension was maintained by the belief that if one side were to launch a direct nuclear attack, the other side would have the capability of launching an equally destructive counterattack, thus assuring mutual destruction. Theoretically, this meant that neither side of the conflict would have any logical reason to launch its weapons, and as long as this balance was upheld, the world would remain safe from nuclear annihilation. But MAD didn't safeguard against rogue nuclear weapons operators, human error, computer error, or terrorist plots, any of which could cause a non-governmental nuclear launch, leading to a counterstrike and thus a worldwide catastrophe.

The Red Scares: Censorship and the Enemy Within

The First Red Scare

In 1917, a Marxist revolutionary group calling themselves Bolsheviks led a successful revolt that overthrew the Russian monarchy and installed a new Communist government. Why should this scare the U.S., thousands of miles away? The idea that Communism could completely wipe out the old way of life was terrifying, especially since Communism was, in the end, just an idea. In the years following the Bolshevik Revolution, Americans thought that a similar revolution might occur in the United States as well, causing the loss of traditional ideas about American norms and freedoms. There was a nationwide backlash against people whose practices seemed to conform to the left wing, communist, or socialist policies of the new Soviet government. Anyone who seemed "infected" by Communist

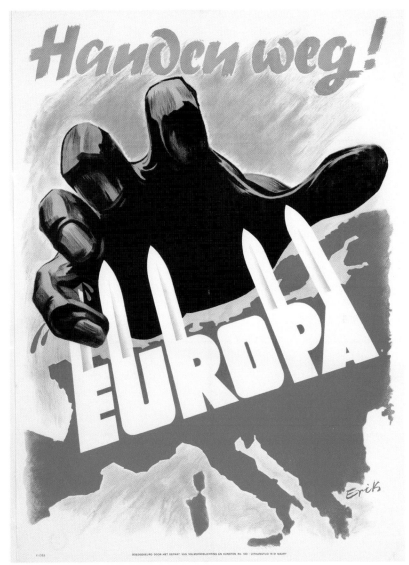

A Nazi propaganda poster from World War II depicting the sinister hand of Communism menacing Europe. The declaration reads, "Hands Off!" This poster was meant to rally German support for Hitler's campaign against Russia.

ideals of nationalizing industry, the power of collective action, stressing communalism over individual's rights, or social justice over personal (or corporate) liberty became a threat to "America." Labor union members and intellectuals particularly fell into this category.

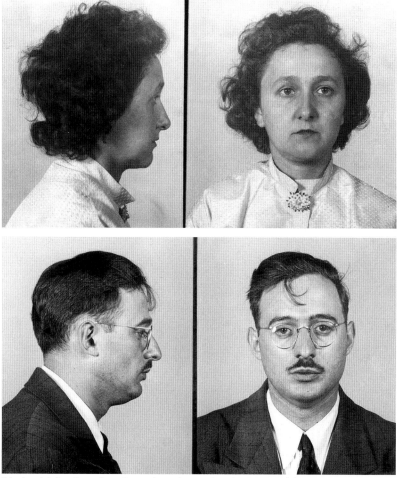

Ethel and Julius Rosenberg (mug shots shown above) were two of the most notorious spies of the Cold War era. They were convicted of nuclear espionage and executed in 1953.

The Second Red Scare

A similar course of events followed the end of World War II. With the rise of Communist Russia—now the leader of the Soviet Union—as a global superpower, the fear of "Reds," or Communists, intensified once again in the U.S. Citizens feared that the Soviets would send spies to infiltrate the government, intelligence agencies such as the CIA, and most horrifyingly, the American nuclear weapons infrastructure. The Soviets did in fact recruit a number of high-level scientists to deliver nuclear secrets during the Cold War. The most widely profiled spies were husband and wife Julius and Ethel Rosenberg from New York. The Rosenbergs were found guilty of supplying nuclear secrets to the Soviets and were executed in June 1953. The possibility of foreign infiltration was very real, and considered extremely dangerous.

McCarthyism and the Invasion Fantasy

Senator Joseph McCarthy made his political career by inciting fear of Communism and by "outing" political enemies as enemies of the State.

In 1950, Senator Joseph McCarthy of Wisconsin controversially claimed to have a list of names of people employed in the State Department who were Communists or Communist sympathizers. While he was never able to prove the truth of his claims, he embarked on an aggressive national campaign accusing and interrogating his political opponents of being linked to Communism. He became a national sensation, but the Senate eventually censured his tactics. Whether or not he ultimately profited from this program of fomenting, or inciting, the fear of Communism, McCarthy accomplished his main task: people were afraid. As with the First Red Scare, many intellectuals, artists, and labor organizers were the targets of attacks.

The number of science fiction narratives dealing with infiltration during this time rose dramatically. Examples of this kind of work include *Invasion of the Body Snatchers* (1956),

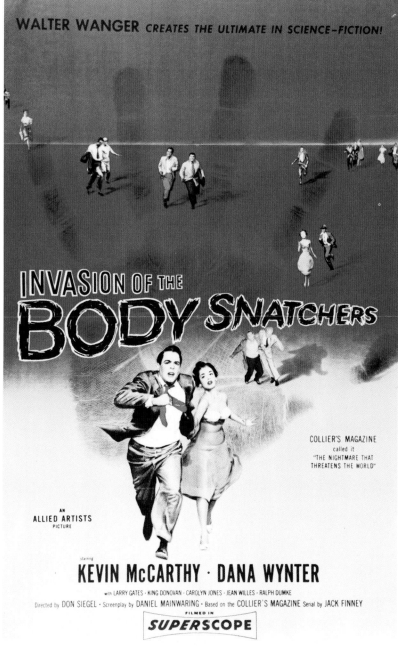

Invasion of the Body Snatchers (1956) was one of many Hollywood films that played to the fears many Americans felt at the idea of foreign infiltration or dangerous contamination by Communism.

The Thing From Another World (1951), and *It Came From Outer Space* (1951). In 1959, Richard Condon published his novel *The Manchurian Candidate*, which told the story of a political insider who is brainwashed by Communists to carry out assassinations. These stories **epitomized** the fears that Americans felt about the invasion of their society and the destruction of their way of life.

Proxy Wars: Containment and the Domino Effect

Korean War

During World War II, the USSR and the United States were allies in the fight against Nazi Germany and Japan. This alliance technically continued after 1945, but soon after Japan's surrender the two nations were vying for influence and control over various parts of the globe formerly controlled by the Axis powers.

One of Japan's colonial possessions was the Korean Peninsula. After Japan surrendered to U.S. forces in 1945, its rule over Korea was officially ended after thirty-five years. One of the postwar projects supported by the Allied powers and the United Nations was to allow Korea to establish its independence through popular elections. To maintain order until these elections could be held, the U.S. and the USSR decided to split the country at the 38th parallel. The Soviets were responsible for stewardship over the north, which it already occupied, and the United States maintained responsibility in the south. This north/south split was meant to be temporary.

The Soviets, however, proved to be resistant to pressure from the United Nations to hold general elections. Instead, a difficult situation emerged: a Communist government was set up in the north, and a democratic government in the south. The two new governments—backed by their respective superpowers—both

U.S. soldiers participate in military exercises in South Korea, 1954.

felt that Korea should be unified, but disagreed over whose authority should prevail. By 1950, the country was embroiled in a devastating civil war. While the Soviets never physically fought in the war, they supported the Chinese and North Korean armies that fought against the American, United Nations, and South Korean forces. Over 1.2 million people—civilians and military—were killed. This Cold War conflict lasted until 1953. The entrenched fighting and great loss of life set the stage for the Vietnam War, and increased tensions between the Americans and Soviets.

Vietnam War

By 1956, the U.S. and the USSR were open rivals. The United States believed that Communism was a threat to world order and freedom, and that its influence had to be stopped. This belief led the U.S. to adopt a policy of containment, which was used to justify military or economic action worldwide in the fight against Soviet Russia. Containment was predicated on a belief in the "domino effect": if a country fell under Soviet control, the surrounding countries were likely to as well.

The doctrines of containment and the domino effect helped rationalize the U.S. decision to fight a long, bloody war in defense of South Vietnam (1954–1975). After more than a century of French and Japanese colonization, Communist groups in Vietnam launched an independence movement that was supported by the Chinese and Soviet governments. The U.S. helped the French and Southern Vietnamese forces resist North Vietnam's attempts to reunify Vietnam under communism. By the 1960s, the U.S. had sent hundreds of thousands of troops to South Asia. After more than eighteen years of conflict, the U.S. evacuated all its forces in 1975. The Vietnam War was unpopular in the United States. It inspired many anti-war protests and the hippie subculture of the 1960s.

Anti-war protests led by students flourished in the '60s and '70s. Here, students at the University of California, Berkeley march against the Vietnam War in 1969.

Ultimately, between three and four million people died in this brutal proxy war, which was the largest and longest of the Cold War era.

Soviet Premier Nikita Khrushchev (right) posing with Cuban president Fidel Castro in 1963.

Worldwide Conflict

A number of other proxy wars and political revolutions occurred during the Cold War. Like Korea and Vietnam, these conflicts were mainly fought between Communist or socialist and democratic groups. Some of these small wars had huge consequences. For example, a Communist uprising in Cuba in 1959 led to the installment of Fidel Castro as the leader of the first Western socialist nation. After the U.S. attempted to remove him from power, Castro gave the Soviets permission to install nuclear missiles in Cuba. The presence of Soviet weapons on Cuban soil resulted in the Cuban Missile Crisis in 1962. For thirteen days, the world seemed to teeter on the brink of all-out nuclear war. Other wars and revolutions occurred in Africa, South America, and Asia, with each contributing to mounting tension around the world.

MAD: The Arms Race

It was known as MAD, or Mutually Assured Destruction. If one side launched nuclear weapons, the other side would counter-launch. Both sides would be totally destroyed.

Therefore, it would be against either side's self-interest to launch its weapons. As long as each side maintained an equal level of nuclear capability and defense, nuclear war was logically impossible.

MAD was a beautifully simple theory, but it had unintended side effects. For one thing, the U.S. and USSR both fought to gain an edge in nuclear capability that might put the opponent at a disadvantage. One way to do this was to develop large numbers of new nuclear weapons: bombs that could be dropped from long-range airplanes; missiles that could be launched from thousands of miles away inside a bunker or a submarine; cruise missiles; air-to-surface missiles; and mortar rounds. The U.S. even developed nuclear bombs that could be delivered by a two-person team, with one person carrying the weapon in a backpack.

For every advance the U.S. made in the number of missiles it could produce with which to intimidate the USSR, the Soviets matched it. On the one hand, this kept the balance of nuclear power stable, ensuring the success of MAD. On the other hand, the globe was rapidly filling up with weapons of mass destruction, each more powerful and deadly than the last. Should they be used in war, the destruction would be total. The Earth would be annihilated by radiation, heat, and then a long **nuclear winter.**

Space: Sputnik, Apollo, and the Giant Leap

"That's one small step for a man, one giant leap for mankind."

— Neil Armstrong, on the occasion of stepping down onto the surface of the moon, July 20, 1969

Sputnik 1

Amazing achievements are often motivated by conflict. The Cold War drove the race to space. The winner of the space race stood to gain a number of benefits by developing space technologies. For example, satellites could be used for spying,

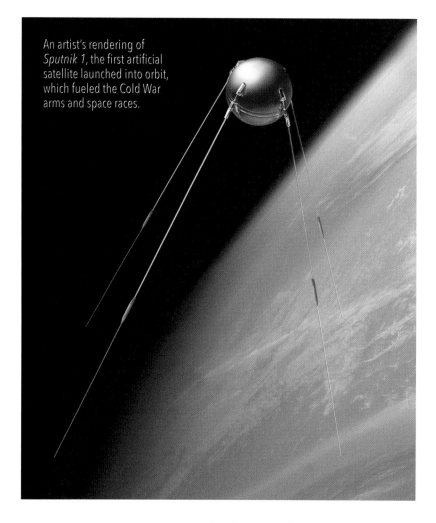

An artist's rendering of *Sputnik 1*, the first artificial satellite launched into orbit, which fueled the Cold War arms and space races.

communications, and potentially for space-based weaponry. More advanced rockets translated to more advanced missiles. The ideas of colonizing and controlling the moon, finding a wealth of resources there, and establishing an unconquerable weapons base there were also enticing.

On October 4, 1957, the Soviet Union launched a tiny metal satellite called *Sputnik 1* into orbit near Earth. Essentially a small metal radio transmitter, it was the first man-made satellite, and it precipitated a major crisis of American confidence. After the launch of *Sputnik 1*, the U.S. invested hundreds of millions of dollars in science and engineering educational programs, as well as its own space program. In 1958, President Eisenhower created the National Aeronautics and Space Administration (NASA), which was to become the world's leading space research and engineering program. Unfortunately, *Sputnik 1* also spurred the U.S. government to increase its nuclear missile inventory.

The first human to orbit the Earth, Soviet cosmonaut Yuri Gagarin, shown here in 1961.

People in Space

In 1961, the Russians dealt the Americans another massive hit in the space race: *Vostok 1* took the first human, a twenty-seven-year-old Soviet pilot named Yuri Gagarin, into orbit. The Soviets were winning the space race.

A month later, the Americans caught up. Alan Shepard went into orbit as part of its first human spaceflight program called Project Mercury. Next came Project Gemini, the second human spaceflight program, which involved multiple astronauts in orbit together. Finally, the Apollo missions began. The goal of the Apollo program was to land a man on the moon, and to do it, according to President Kennedy, before 1970. After the initial momentum achieved by the Soviet space program, the Americans were motivated to make great strides. In 1969, astronauts Neil Armstrong and Buzz Aldrin were the first humans to walk on the moon. A total of six Apollo missions sent astronauts to the moon. The Soviets, as it turned out, never left low-Earth orbit.

Photo of American astronaut Buzz Aldrin during the first moon landing, 1969.

Space and Science Fiction

Of all the Cold War events, the space race was the most directly related to science fiction themes, but it also inspired many new speculative fiction trends. The possibility of walking on other **celestial** bodies was not just a possibility but a reality. The idea of exploring the farthest reaches of the universe was alluring, and the technology required to do it was also a source of fascination. The Apollo missions helped spur the development of computers, spacecraft, and advanced communications equipment.

Tearing Down the Wall: The End of the Cold War

Gorbachev the Reformer

The Cold War couldn't last forever. When Mikhail Gorbachev was elected as the head of state of the Soviet Union in 1989, it was clear that the Soviet economy was in need of serious reform. While the Soviets had poured money into their military and defense infrastructure to keep up with the United States in the arms race, basic services and institutions had suffered.

Until the late 1980s, when Gorbachev began to enact major economic changes, the Soviet economy had followed the nationwide centralized economic plans of the Communist Party leaders in the form of Five Year Plans. Through these plans, the Soviet economy was controlled and predetermined by the state, rather than being relatively unregulated and subject to market forces, such as was the case in Western capitalist systems. Gorbachev introduced two major changes to this system: *perestroika*, or "restructuring," and *glasnost*, or "openness." Gorbachev wanted to bolster the centralized Soviet economy, but he inadvertently triggered the end of the Soviet Union.

The End of the Soviet Union

As citizens of the Soviet Union began to exercise their new freedom to criticize the government, they quickly began to call for independence from Moscow. All of the nations and territories that Russia had annexed after World War II now wanted out. Instability and rivalry from within the Communist Party combined with increasing pressure from each of the satellite nations and led inevitably to the end of the Soviet Union. In 1991, a **coup** temporarily unseated Gorbachev, and when he came back to his post as head of state, he had lost much of his power to command. On December 25, 1991, Gorbachev announced his resignation. The USSR dissolved.

Perestroika and Glasnost

Gorbachev's proposed perestroika and glasnost were radical and controversial in Russia. Gorbachev wanted to tread the fine line between social freedoms—many of which, such as the freedom to criticize the government or the freedom to own an industrial company, had not been seen in the Soviet Union since before the days of Lenin—and socialist planning. By extending freedoms to citizens of the USSR, Gorbachev hoped to change the social and cultural fabric of the population, to combat rampant alcoholism, depression, low-quality manufacturing, corruption in government and business, and a lack of internal motivation. He recognized that the Soviet Union needed to upgrade its technological and industrial powers. Gorbachev understood that economic progress had to happen alongside a reduction in Cold War tensions, which meant that he had to become allied with formerly **antagonistic** leaders such as United States President Ronald Reagan and United Kingdom Prime Minister Margaret Thatcher.

The Cold War winds down as Soviet leader Mikhael Gorbachev (left) negotiates with U.S. President Ronald Reagan in 1987.

A young boy helps take down the Berlin Wall on November 12, 1989.

Breaking Through to a New Era: The Fall of the Berlin Wall

What did this mean, in practical terms? The central committee of Soviets had wielded power over most of Eastern Europe, including East Germany and the eastern half of the city of Berlin. To restrict East Berliners from fleeing the harsh Soviet-dominated political climate for the freedom of the West, a high wall was built to separate the two halves of the city. The Berlin Wall was a tangible example of the kind of hold the Soviet government had over its territories, and the totalitarian authority that the central committee employed. When the political landscape began to change in late 1989, the East German government officially allowed its citizens to travel freely to the West. On November 9, 1989, thousands of Berliners from both sides converged on the Wall and, in a show of exuberance seldom seen on the world stage, they began to demolish it with hammers. Images of the fall of the Berlin Wall reverberated around the world, signaling a new era. Would the new era be a time of peace?

TWO

The Life of Ray Bradbury

Early Life: Waukegan, Tucson, and L.A.

Ray Douglas Bradbury was born in the small town of Waukegan, Illinois, on August 22, 1920. In the introduction to *The Ray Bradbury Companion*, Bradbury claims to "have what might be called almost total recall back to the hour of my birth." He remembers his own birth as a traumatic event that he says gave him nightmares as an infant. This originary trauma was the basis for Bradbury's short story "The Small Assassin."

Bradbury was the third son of Leonard Spaulding Bradbury and Esther Marie Bradbury. His older brothers, Leonard and Samuel, were twins born in 1916. Ray Bradbury never met his brother Samuel, who died in 1918 at the age of two. In 1926, the Bradburys had a daughter named Elizabeth, who died in 1927, seven months after her birth.

Ray Bradbury's grandfather and great-grandfather published newspapers in Illinois, which might be the first of many early signs that Bradbury was destined for a life of letters. When

Bradbury was captivated by the magic of Hollywood and spent many hours in the movie theater watching silent films, including *The Mask of Zorro*, starring Douglas Fairbanks.

Bradbury was young, his father worked for the Waukegan Bureau of Power and Light as a telephone lineman. His mother was enthralled by the movies, and she was eager to share her love of films with her young son. In fact, Bradbury's middle name was given to him in honor of Douglas Fairbanks, the silent film actor perhaps best remembered for his roles in *The Mark of Zorro* and *Robin Hood*. His mother took him to see *The*

Hunchback of Notre Dame when he was three years old, and the image of the actor Lon Chaney as the misshapen Quasimodo made a lasting impression on the young Bradbury. He was also fascinated by the images of dinosaurs in the 1925 film *The Lost World*, which is based on Arthur Conan Doyle's illustrated novel. In the introduction to the book *They Came from Outer Space*, Bradbury remembers being sent to the movie theaters to bring home his "maniac" mother by writing, "More often than not the son forgot why he had come and stayed with mom for one more rerun."

Bradbury's love affair with books began early on. At the age of six, Bradbury was enchanted by L. Frank Baum's *Oz* books and a book of fairy tales, *Once Upon a Time*, given to him by his aunt Neva, who shared his enthusiasm for fantastic stories. He also read Greek, Roman, and Norse mythology when he was very young. He especially relished *Buck Rogers*, *Flash Gordon*, and *Prince Valiant* comic books, as well as Edgar Rice Burroughs's *Tarzan* stories. Bradbury discovered the library when he was nine or ten, and spent many ecstatic nights there immersed in stories. An imaginative child, he was excited by the many wonders he encountered during his childhood, which included radio programs, museums, magic, and the circus.

When Bradbury's father lost his job in Waukegan due to the Great Depression, the family moved to Tucson, Arizona, for the second time in 1932 (they'd lived there for a six-month period between 1926 and 1927.) In Tucson, Bradbury, who'd always loved radio, hung out at the local radio station after school and eventually wrangled his way onto the air reading comic strips. He was an avid collector of comics and loved reading them on the radio. Better still, the young Bradbury remembered being paid in tickets to the local cinema, "My pay was free tickets to see *King Kong*, *Murders in the Wax Museum*, and *The Mummy* ... I've never had better income in my life since." It was also during this time that his parents gave him a toy typewriter for Christmas, on which he wrote some of his first stories. The Bradbury family lived in Tucson for about a year before returning to Waukegan.

In 1934, the Bradburys moved to Los Angeles, California, and rented an apartment in Hollywood. Bradbury attended Los Angeles High School. Hollywood was the center of the American film industry at the time, and Bradbury—who'd always loved movies and acting—joined his high school's drama club. He continued writing and, for a while, dictated his stories to a girl he'd met who lived next door. She was willing to type his stories for him until he could save up to buy his own typewriter in 1937.

Around this time, Bradbury joined a group of science fiction fans called the Los Angeles Science Fiction League, and started sending his stories out to magazines for publication. None of them were accepted, but by the time Bradbury graduated high school, he was definitely on his way. He immersed himself in lots of great writing—his tastes had been expanded, thanks to a creative writing course—wrote every day, published stories in fan magazines, and met influential people in the science fiction world.

Literary Influences

Many of today's writers talk about what inspired them to write, what their writing routines are like, and who and what their influences are. The late novelist David Foster Wallace described his writing process in a way that seems to apply to many writers, saying, "I get to use pretty much everything I've ever learned or thought about." A lifetime of experience is condensed and channeled into the creation of a poem, short story, or novel. Writers are typically great readers, collecting **innumerable** pieces of other writers' life experiences as rewards for their reading. Ray Bradbury was not only a tremendous reader, but also a keen observer of many aspects of life. He seemed to take everything in, and released much into his writing.

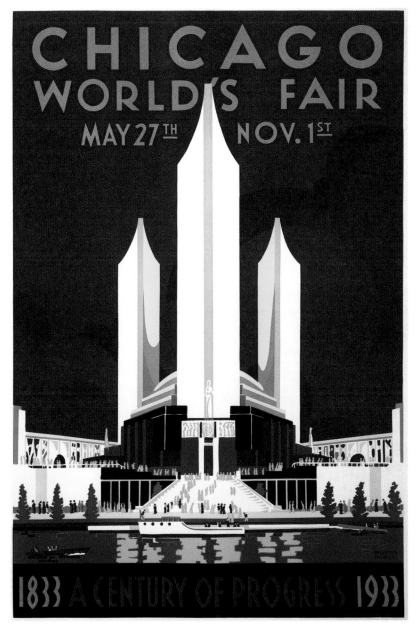

Bradbury was particularly influenced by the women in his life, including his aunt Neva, who took him to the Chicago World's Fair in 1933.

Bradbury was particularly influenced by the women in his family, who exposed him to films, books, and cultural events. His aunt Neva introduced him to fantasy fiction, and also took him to Chicago for the World's Fair in the summer of 1933. Called "A Century of Progress," the fair commemorated the 100-year anniversary of Chicago's incorporation as a city. The purpose of the fair was "to demonstrate to an international audience the nature and significance of scientific discoveries, the methods of achieving them, and the changes which their application has wrought in industry and in living conditions." Bradbury's mother's penchant for silent films rubbed off on him, and the films he saw with her as a child shaped his later writing. For example, the deformed body of Quasimodo from the film *The Hunchback of Notre Dame* is reconfigured

in Bradbury's 1990 novel *A Graveyard for Lunatics*. The novel is a mystery about a fictional screenwriter—based on Bradbury's own experience writing for the movies—working for a Hollywood studio in 1954. His mother also introduced him to Edgar Allan Poe's stories by reading them aloud to her son while he was sick for a month with whooping cough.

Jules Verne, author of *20,000 Leagues Under the Sea*, was a huge influence on Bradbury.

Bradbury later trained himself in the short story form by reading such masters as John Steinbeck, Ernest Hemingway, John Collier, Willa Cather, Edith Wharton, Eudora Welty, Herman Melville, Rudyard Kipling, and Charles Dickens. When asked about this, he replied, "I read every short story by every American writer over the years ... I pretty well educated myself in the short story in every country in the world. If you're going to write them, you better know them."

However, identifying a writer's own literary influences is never just a matter of listing such **canonical** writers. After all, most people with a formal education have read them. For writers of Bradbury's generation and even today, non-canonical literary works, genre fiction, television, and popular movies tend to be much more important influences.

As sharp observers of the world around them, writers can be both consciously and unconsciously influenced by their surroundings. This sense of place often contributes to a writer's unique voice. In Bradbury's case, the small-town culture of Waukegan, Illinois where he grew up features prominently in his novels *Dandelion Wine*, *Something Wicked This Way Comes*, *Farewell Summer*, and the short story collection *Summer Morning, Summer Night*.

Living in Los Angeles, Bradbury was in a perfect position to rub shoulders with many influential people in the world of science fiction, including Robert Heinlein and Leigh Brackett. Heinlein is one of the most influential science fiction writers in the history of the genre, and Bradbury attended one of his writing classes. Brackett wrote stories, novels, and screenplays, and worked closely with Bradbury on his stories. Bradbury was also an active participant in the science fiction fan subculture, or "fandom," that began in the late 1920s and blossomed in the 1940s. Fandom is extremely important to the history of science fiction. Even as early as the 1940s, SF fans held conventions where fans and authors could meet to talk about the genre.

Robert Heinlein, L. Sprague de Camp, and Isaac Asimov (from left) are extremely influential writers from the Golden Age of Science Fiction. Robert Heinlein was a mentor to Bradbury at the beginning of his writing career.

Fans also wrote their own science fiction and published their pieces in magazines called "fanzines." Bradbury often contributed to other people's fanzines, and published his own, *Futuria Fantasia,* in 1939.

Writing for a Living

1941 was an important year for Bradbury. He wrote fifty-two stories, and although he sold only three of them, he decided to make writing his full-time job. In interviews he would later recall his modest lifestyle, saying, "I was being paid twenty to forty dollars a story, by the pulp magazines. High on the hog was hardly my way of life. I had to sell at least one story, or better two, each month in order to survive my hot-dog, hamburger, trolley-car-fare life." In addition to selling science fiction stories, he sold mysteries to pulp magazines such as *Flynn's Detective Fiction* and *New Detective*.

Although Bradbury was able to support himself by writing, it took a while before higher-paying magazines such as *Harper's* and the *Atlantic Monthly* accepted his work. He was eager to break into more mainstream magazines, not only because it would mean higher pay, but also because he wanted to reach a wider audience. Bradbury in fact once consulted a psychologist about his desire to be a famous writer. The doctor advised him to go to the library and read up on famous authors such as Charles Dickens and Honoré de Balzac—writers whose fame was a long time in the making.

Bradbury's strategy for becoming a famous author was to write every day and submit his works to as many magazines as possible. His writing process began with word associations and metaphors, which he then developed into a story. As he once explained, "I simply got out of bed each morning, walked to my desk, and put down any word or series of words that happened along in my head. I would then take arms against the word, or for it, and bring on an assortment of characters to weigh the word and show me its meaning in my own life." Bradbury wrote in this way for most of his life. By allowing his subconscious to do the work of providing ideas, Bradbury said he never suffered from writer's block.

In addition to sending his works out to science fiction, mystery, and other literary magazines, Bradbury would send his stories to magazines that didn't normally publish fiction. This strategy paid off when *Gourmet*—a magazine devoted to food and wine—published Bradbury's short story "Dandelion Wine," which later became part of his novel of the same name. By the mid 1940s, Bradbury's broke into the major magazines, and his short stories were also being published in the popular compilation, *Best American Short Stories*.

Marguerite Susan McClure

Fans of Bradbury's works owe a huge debt of gratitude to his wife, Marguerite Susan McClure. Although Bradbury was writing for a living when he married Marguerite, he wasn't earning enough money to support a family. However, if he were to take another job, he wouldn't have the time to write as much as he did. Marguerite believed deeply in her husband's writing, and instead of sacrificing Bradbury's career, she went to work every day at an advertising agency. In the early years of their marriage, hers was the primary income for the household. This was not at all common at the time, as women rarely worked outside of the house. Marguerite's support gave Bradbury the freedom to write the stories that have made him one of the most successful and influential American writers of the twentieth century.

Marriage and Mainstream Success

In 1946, twenty-six-year-old Bradbury met twenty-four-year-old Marguerite McClure while she was working at Fowler Brothers bookstore in Los Angeles. Marguerite recognized Bradbury as a local pulp magazine writer, but the long trench coat he was wearing on that hot Los Angeles afternoon sent up red flags for her. Books had been disappearing from Fowler's at the time, and she thought he might be a shoplifter. They started talking, however, and her fears were allayed. They discovered that they shared an interest in literature and had similar views. He asked her out for coffee, but Marguerite suggested they go for cocktails instead.

Marguerite was the only woman Bradbury ever dated, and they married a year later. Bradbury insisted that she couldn't have wanted him for his money—he didn't have any. In his speech at the National Book Awards in 2000, he said, "We had a ceremony at an Episcopal Church and I put $5 in an envelope and handed it to the minister. He said, 'What's this?' I said, 'That's your pay for the ceremony today.' He said, 'You're a writer, aren't you?' I said, 'Yes.' He said, 'Then you're going to need this.'"

Bradbury and Marguerite had four daughters in all: Susan in 1949, Ramona in 1951, Bettina in 1955, and Alexandra in 1958. Having children temporarily complicated the money situation for the couple, but Bradbury's writing was soon to pay off in a much bigger way than ever before.

Bradbury published his first book, a collection of horror stories called *Dark Carnival*, in 1947. Shortly afterward, a man named Don Congdon noticed Bradbury's work and became his literary agent. Congdon and Bradbury would continue to work together for over fifty years.

The idea for Bradbury's first novel, *The Martian Chronicles*, came out of a dinner conversation he had in New York with Congdon and an editor at Doubleday Books named

Walter Bradbury (no relation to Ray). Bradbury had taken a Greyhound bus to New York to try to sell his short stories. He wasn't having much luck until Walter suggested he take the Martian stories he'd published in pulp magazines and piece them together into a novel. Bradbury, who'd recently imagined writing a book like Sherwood Anderson's *Winesburg, Ohio* and setting it on Mars, leapt at the idea. Walter told him to write an outline for the novel and bring it to his office at Doubleday.

Ray Bradbury at the height of his career in the late 1950s.

The following day, he was paid an advance of $750 for *The Martian Chronicles*, and an additional $750 advance for *The Illustrated Man*—a combined total equal to over $16,000 in today's dollars. Bradbury's career was about to launch into the stratosphere.

Published in 1950, *The Martian Chronicles* took off when the famous novelist Christopher Isherwood reviewed it in *Tomorrow* magazine. Bradbury met Isherwood at a book signing in Santa Monica and gave him a copy of *The Martian Chronicles*. Isherwood, who had recently been hired to review books for *Tomorrow*, decided to make Bradbury's novel his first review. Bradbury was already fairly well known by science fiction fans, but Isherwood's review introduced Bradbury's writing to a much wider audience. *The Illustrated Man*, a short story collection in which every story develops out of a tattoo, further boosted Bradbury's appeal when it appeared in 1951. *Fahrenheit 451* followed in 1953. And by the time *Dandelion*

Wine—a semi-autobiographical novel based on his experiences growing up in a small town—appeared in 1957, Bradbury had completely broken out of the small world of pulp science fiction and mystery magazines and into the much larger realm of mainstream literary fiction.

Later Achievements

In his later work, Bradbury moved away from the science fiction writing that made him famous, but with which he never fully identified, choosing instead to explore other themes and genres. He continued to write every day for the rest of his life. With more than 500 published works to his credit, Bradbury's creative output was nothing less then astounding. In addition to his many short stories and novels, Bradbury wrote and produced stage plays, television and film scripts—including the screenplay for John Huston's 1956 adaptation of *Moby Dick*—books for children, and poetry collections. Many of his works have been adapted for television and film, including *Something Wicked This Way Comes*, *The Illustrated Man*, and *The Martian Chronicles*. *Fahrenheit 451* was turned into a film, a play, and briefly, an unsuccessful musical. Several of his short stories also appear as comics in the 2003 book *The Best of Ray Bradbury: The Graphic Novel*.

Ironically, the man who could envision alien worlds in vivid detail, imagine machines that could do the inexplicable, and explore the affect of technology on the human psyche wanted nothing to do with computers or the Internet. When *The Martian Chronicles* was turned into a CD-ROM game, Bradbury supported the project, but was completely uninterested in playing it. He was quoted as saying, "I don't understand this whole thing about computers and the superhighway. Who wants to be in touch with all of those people?"

Fans from all walks of life, from architects and urban planners to scientists and engineers, have turned to Bradbury

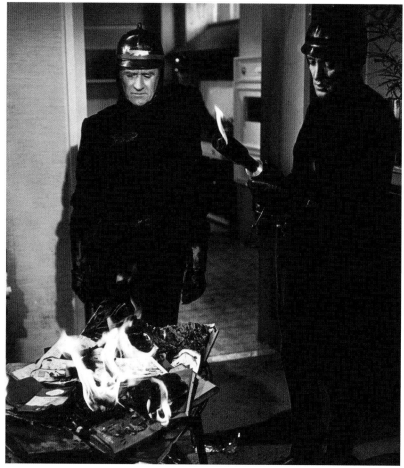

Firemen burning books in the 1966 film version of *Fahrenheit 451*, directed by François Truffaut.

for inspiration. Officials from the cities of San Diego and Glendale asked him to help rejuvenate their downtown areas by designing playful, dynamic shopping centers. According to Bradbury, his story "The Veldt" planted the seeds for the development of virtual reality machines, and when a "bright Sony inventor read about my seashell radios [in *Fahrenheit 451*], he invented the Walkman." For the 1964 World's Fair in Queens, New York, Bradbury wrote an eighteen-minute script about the history of America for the U.S. pavilion. Nearly twenty years later, Bradbury developed the storyline and wrote the script for Epcot, which became a star attraction at his good friend Walt Disney's theme park, Disney World. Long an advocate for space travel, particularly to Mars, Bradbury was among the first people to comment on the landing of the unmanned space probe *Pathfinder* in 1997.

Bradbury in a NASA control room, 1979: His fascination with space exploration persisted throughout his life.

Although Bradbury's success may have been a long time in coming, he has been well lauded for his many contributions to science fiction and speculative fiction. He has won numerous awards for individual short stories, novels, poetry, and screenplays, as well as several lifetime achievement accolades. After receiving the O. Henry Prize in both 1947 and 1948, he went on to receive the 1954 National Institute of Arts and Letters Award for Contribution to American Literature, the World Fantasy Award for lifetime achievement in 1977, and the Grand Master Nebula Award from the Science Fiction and Fantasy Writers of America in 1988. He was conferred a medal for "Distinguished Contribution to American Letters"

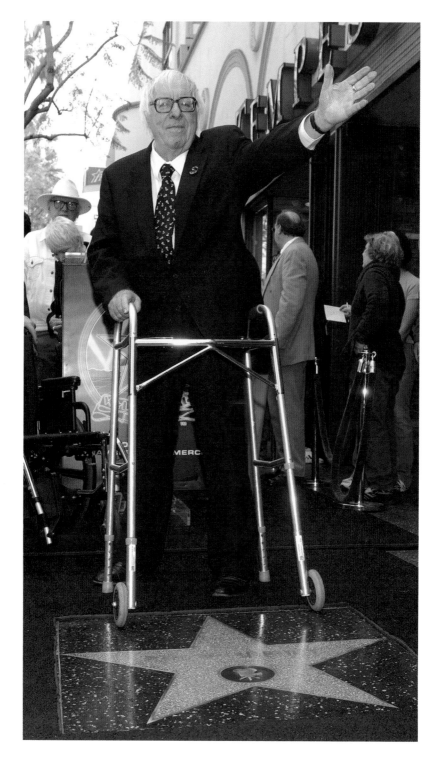

from the National Book Foundation in 2000, the National Medal of the Arts in 2004, and received a special citation for a distinguished career from the Pulitzer Board in 2007. In 1971, the crew of *Apollo 15* named an impact crater on the moon Dandelion Crater in honor of Bradbury's novel *Dandelion Wine*. Bradbury's awards extended to include his televisions and film work. In 1963, he received an Academy Award nomination for best short film for *Icarus Montgolfier Wright*, and he won an Emmy for his teleplay of *The Halloween Tree* in 1994. The Science Fiction and Fantasy Writers of America created The Ray Bradbury Award for screenwriting in his honor. He even has a star on Hollywood Walk of Fame.

Ray Bradbury died on June 5, 2012 at the age of ninety-one True to his word, Bradbury wrote every day until his death. His work continues to be an enormous influence on science fiction writers and readers. While his stories and books are widely read and discussed in high schools, they are also still powerful and controversial enough to be challenged and even banned. Throughout his stories and across all genres, Bradbury warned people against sacrificing their morals, aesthetics, and critical thought by becoming too dependent on science and technology. By reading Bradbury's work, today's readers can both learn about the past and prepare for the future.

When he was eighty-one years old, Ray Bradbury received a star on the Hollywood Walk of Fame in recognition of his enormous contribution to film.

THREE

The Martian Chronicles

"What has this man from Illinois done, I ask myself when closing the pages of his book, that episodes from the conquest of another planet fill me with horror and loneliness?"

— Jorge Luis Borges, Preface to *Crónicas Marcianas*, the 1954 Spanish edition of *The Martian Chronicles*

Writing and Publishing *The Martian Chronicles*

Ray Bradbury was a struggling young writer in 1949 when he traveled to New York City to pitch his collection of short stories to any publisher that would listen. He was repeatedly rejected by publishers who wanted a novel, not a story collection. When editor Walter Bradbury from Doubleday suggested he arrange his stories set on Mars into a "novel" called *The Martian Chronicles,* Bradbury agreed. The book was published the following year to great critical praise, launching and cementing Ray Bradbury's position as an acclaimed American author.

Versions of Futures Past

Jorge Luis Borges, circa 1968.

The content of *The Martian Chronicles* has changed from its original 1950 publication, as it saw revision and translation in subsequent editions. The Spanish language edition in 1954 includes a preface by Jorge Luis Borges, a famous Argentinian author and critic. The United Kingdom version, released in 1951, was called *The Silver Locusts*. A revised edition in 1997 contained more substantial changes, replacing "Way in the Middle of the Air"–which was relevant to the racial tensions surrounding the civil rights movement in the 1950s, but would have seemed dated to later audiences–with two other short stories, "The Fire Balloons" and "The Wilderness." This edition also added thirty-one years to the dates in the stories' titles: *The Martian Chronicles* was originally meant to begin in 1999, and by 1997, it was clear that there weren't going to be any human colonies on Mars within the next two years.

This book refers to the original 1950 edition of *The Martian Chronicles*, not because it is inherently better than the others, but because it best reflects Bradbury's intentions for the text in the era after World War II.

Mars as an Object of Fascination

Ever since Italian astronomer Giovanni Schiaparelli observed what he called *canali* (Italian for "channels" or "grooves") on the surface of Mars in 1877, the red planet has been a place of mystery and exciting possibilities. The lines that Schiaparelli and others saw on the surface of the planet at the time took hold in the popular imagination as evidence of intelligent life on Mars: The lines were surely canals or roads of some sort.

Nearly a century later, when Ray Bradbury was busy imagining the human colonization of Mars, much more was known about the planet, but many questions still remained. In the decades following the publication of *The Martian Chronicles,* both the USSR and the U.S. funded programs to send unmanned probes to Mars. The projects were scientifically motivated, but they also represented an area of space exploration upon which political **rhetoric** could be based. Bradbury was clearly not interested in a technical recapitulation of how to get to Mars, nor was he interested in providing a blueprint for the practicalities of colonizing a distant planet. His tales use humans' original fascination with Mars as a place of mystery and power, and they pay little attention to the "science." For this and other reasons, Bradbury was able to insist that he wasn't, in fact, a science fiction writer at all.

Events from Bradbury's Life that Shaped *The Martian Chronicles*

History is crucial to an understanding of a work of literature. That is not to say that we should reduce a book to the author's biography, but a more complete analysis of the text can be made by referring to historical events and influences. In the case of the writing and publication of *The Martian Chronicles*, the events in Bradbury's life that directly contributed to the stories might be his childhood in Waukegan, Illinois, and his reading

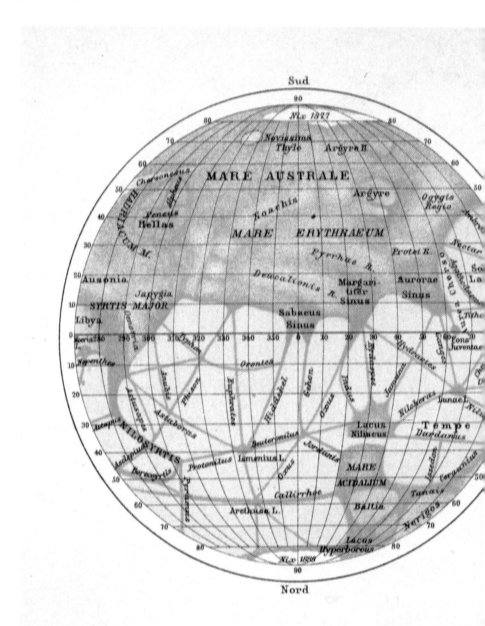

Giovanni Schiaparelli's 1888 map of Mars depicting the canali
and what were thought to be oceans (see "Mare Australe",
the Australian Sea, at the top right).

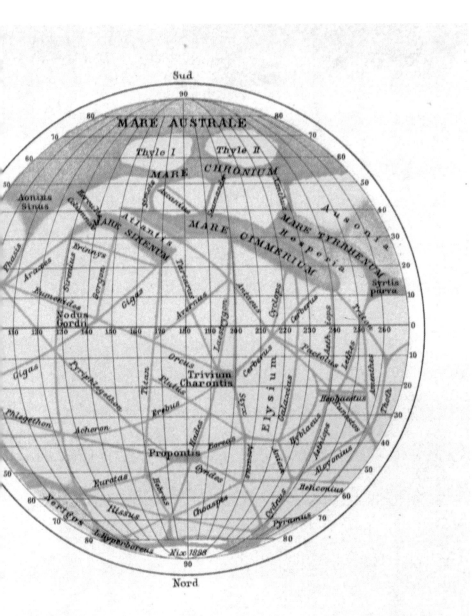

Carte d'ensemble de la planète Mars
avec ses lignes sombres non doublées
observées pendant les six oppositions de 1877-1888
par J.V. Schiaparelli.

of the novel/story collection *Winesburg, Ohio* by Sherwood Anderson. Both of these events brought Bradbury closer to the heart of American small-town life, which is vividly depicted in his own novel/story collection. It is against this depiction of the American heartland that Mars—and the anxieties of the Cold War—can be set.

Waukegan, Illinois is decidedly an American small town. Bradbury spent his early childhood there, and he remained sentimental about it his entire life. It appears in his fiction as "Green Town, IL," providing the setting for major works such as *Dandelion Wine* and *Something Wicked This Way Comes*.

Bradbury's hometown of Waukegan, Illinois.

In *The Martian Chronicles*, it appears in "The Third Expedition" as the small town that appears like everyone's hometown, the image of perfect American Midwest charm, calm, and happiness. Of course, in the story that charm conceals the sinister plot to murder the space explorers, but Bradbury's heartfelt connection to the place of his childhood is clear nonetheless.

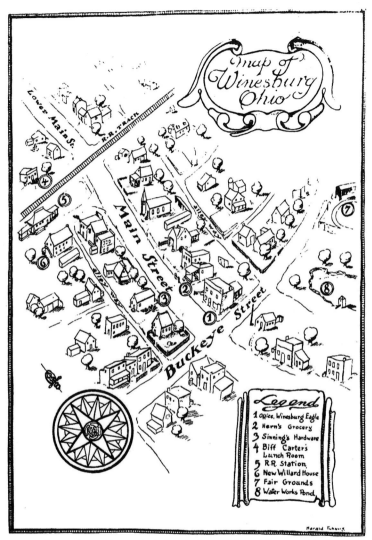

A map of Winesburg, Ohio included in the first edition of Sherwood Anderson's book, which greatly influenced Bradbury's writing.

Supplementing his love of the American small town was his reading of *Winesburg, Ohio* by Sherwood Anderson, which Bradbury credits as a major influence on *The Martian Chronicles*. The resemblance is notable. Both texts are collections of loosely related short stories, and both feature the aura of small-town America as it disappears or evolves.

Plot Synopsis

The Martian Chronicles is a collection of loosely connected short stories that narrates the first human expeditions to Mars, the ensuing large-scale colonization of the planet, the nuclear war that destroys Earth, and the subsequent abandonment of Mars by its Earth colonists. Many of the stories were published in other venues before Bradbury collected them in 1950, and while there are several recurring characters, the stories can be read independently of each other.

The overarching narrative is presented chronologically, with each story title beginning with a date: "January 1999: Rocket Summer" and "February 1999: Ylla," for example. The first seven stories give the account of the first three tentative exploratory expeditions to Mars from Earth, which all result in the total annihilation of their crews. These stories are very different in tone. In "Ylla," the **eponymous** female Martian protagonist has telepathic dream-visions of an impending visit from an otherworldly (Earth)man named Nathaniel York. Ylla's husband, a brutal and jealous Martian, intercepts the rocket when it does actually land and murders the astronauts before his wife can see them. "Ylla" is one of the only stories in the collection that offers the reader a sense of Martian life. Ylla and her husband, Mr. K, live in a villa surrounded by "crystal pillars" from which "a gentle rain sprang ... cooling the scorched air, falling gently on her." The chair in which Ylla reclines "moved to take her shape even as she moved." The doors of the villa are triangular, and they cook meat in a fire table full of "silver lava."

Mr. K spends his time reading epic tales of ancient battles. The description of epic tales and a peaceful, cloistered life among misting pillars serves to create an atmosphere **redolent** of ancient Greece, except that the technology the Martians employ is not mechanical but natural: flaming, **aqueous**, gaseous. When Ylla is chilly, her husband hands her a phial

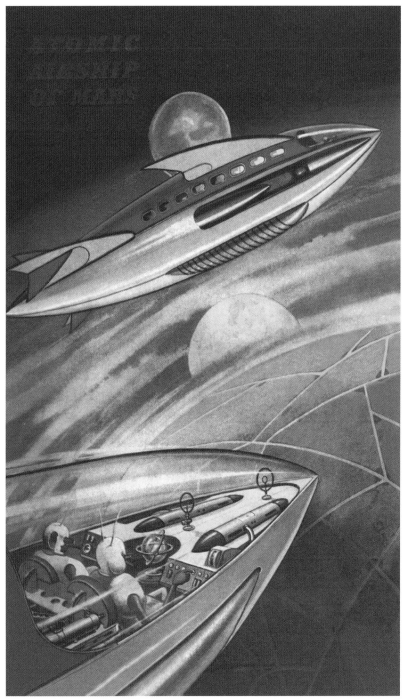

An early twentieth century imaginative depiction of a trip to Mars.

from which "a liquid poured, turned to blue mist, settled about her neck, quivering." This liquid is her scarf. The naturalistic technologies and quiet lifestyle of the Martians contrast violently against the metal rocket ship making its way through space toward Mars. The **juxtaposition** of ancient wisdom and harmony on Mars with futuristic technology and violence from Earth is reiterated throughout the rest of the text.

In an almost comical turn, "The Earth Men" tells the story of the humans' second ill-fated expedition to Mars. Believing the astronauts to be insane because they claim to come from Earth, the native Martians kill the entire expedition crew. Because Martians have the telepathic power to make other minds hallucinate, insanity is dangerous because it could, in effect, be contagious. Thus, the only sure way to guard against untruths becoming mass hallucinations, according to the Martian psychiatric thinking, is to kill the person who is labeled "insane." A Martian psychiatrist shoots the astronauts and then shoots himself when the rocket—the hallucination created by the "mental patients"—doesn't disappear. He believes that he has been infected by the insanity, and so cures himself.

In "The Third Expedition," a haunting tale of dreams and loss, the Americans (all the colonists are from the U.S.) encounter a Martian town that closely resembles their hometowns on Earth. Soon, long-lost loved ones, some of whom died years before, appear and embrace the astronauts. Each crew member is brought to his childhood home, where the hallucinations become more convincing. That night, the Martians, who have been weaving the telepathic spell, kill the entire crew.

In "—And the Moon Be Still as Bright," the final expeditionary force before the main colonization of Mars occurs is almost wiped out by one of its own crew members, an archaeologist named Spender. Spender appreciates the profound beauty and wisdom of the ancient culture they encounter on Mars and worries that it will be destroyed by the **callous** humans. By attacking the crew and making his plans to sabotage future missions clear, Spender forces Captain Wilder, Hathaway, and Sam Parkhill, who all reappear in later stories, to kill him. Despite his death, Spender's warning against humans violating Mars in the same way that they exploited and destroyed Earth resonates throughout *The Martian Chronicles*.

The first expeditions highlight the complexity and mysterious powers of the native Martians, including alien technologies for heating and cooling, weapons that propel deadly bees instead of bullets, and telepathic communication and methods of psychological manipulation. These powers carry through the text, even after the Martians have been eradicated by disease and violence.

The middle section of the book, from August 2001 until November 2005, tells stories about the human colonization of Mars on a larger scale. Settlements are built and various programs offer incentives for people to develop the desolate red landscape. "June 2003: Way in the Middle of the Air" describes the mass migration of African Americans to Mars on rockets they have collectively financed and built in secret. Their **ostensive** purpose is to escape the racial oppression and violence of the United States and establish their own communitarian society. Alluding to Edgar Allan Poe's "The Fall of the House of Usher," the protagonist of "April 2005: Usher II" takes revenge on American censorship officials who participated in book burning and cultural purification. In November 2005, the colonists learn about the nuclear war that breaks out on Earth. Worried about their loved ones, they board rockets and return to Earth, leaving a few stragglers on Mars to fend for themselves.

The final section, from April 2026 until October 2026, relates the death of the last remaining colonist, and the arrival of a family of Americans that came to Mars to escape the nuclear holocaust and rapidly deteriorating environmental conditions on Earth. The new colonists hope to rebuild the human race, this time avoiding the global violence and cultural corruption that plagued the previous century.

Cultural Context

The Golden Age of Science Fiction

Science fiction and speculative fiction from the mid-twentieth century focused closely on questions of human identity, relationships between humans and technology, and possibilities of the end of human civilizations. At the particular moment in science fiction history when Bradbury published *The Martian Chronicles*, science fiction was considered a literary sub-genre. SF was presented in sensationalist magazines with **lurid** covers and aimed mostly toward an adolescent audience. However, science fiction works by writers such as Bradbury, Isaac Asimov, and Robert Heinlein began to garner attention from the mainstream literary establishment in the late 1940s and the 1950s.

Science fiction at this time drew on the culture of technological futurism that was jump-started by post-war inventions, as well as on the philosophical possibilities of technological and interplanetary speculation. In 1949, Heinlein published *Red Planet*, a novel about young colonial students on Mars who encounter an ancient race of Martians with mystical religious and cultural practices. The following year, Asimov's *I, Robot*, a collection of stories centered on the theme of humans' and **androids'** relationship to each other, was published to popular acclaim in 1950.

Technology vs. Humanism

Not since the Industrial Revolution had technology played such a key role in culture and politics as it did in the decades following World War II. While there was a great deal of anxiety surrounding nuclear stockpiling in the mid-twentieth century, technology and futurism were increasingly used to lend a glamorous **veneer** to new products. The atomic bomb was invented in 1945, and the hydrogen bomb was produced in 1952. Many new products were invented around the same time, such as digital computers (1942), microwave ovens (1946), super glue (1951), bar codes (1952), synthesizers (1953), Teflon pans and solar cells (1954), and tetracycline (a broad-spectrum antibiotic) and fiber optic cables (1955). This was also, of course, the time when television sets began to appear in many American households. In an era defined by rapidly advancing technology, the future seemed to be in the present, and hard science and science fiction appeared to be merging.

An issue of *Planet Stories* with bright, exciting images, which appealed to the young target audience.

From the outset of this optimistic futurism, the Bomb lurked in the background as a constant reminder that technology can destroy life as well as improve it. Science fiction responded by taking a less sensationalist and more philosophical turn. The sinister character of technology became—and remains— a favorite topic for science fiction writers. The idea that technology can turn against us, or transform us into something other than human, is a recurrent theme. If computers become extensions of our brains, where is the boundary between my

Marjorie Adams, Miss Chicago of 1950-51, demonstrating a General Electric TV at Chicago's Merchandise Mart in 1952. This television had a three inch screen.

human "self" and the outer world? Will technology ultimately corrode or destroy what it means to be a human being? Conversely, what can a serious look at technology teach us about who we are and our place in the universe? Bradbury poses questions like these throughout his texts.

Major Characters

Because *The Martian Chronicles* is a collection of loosely connected short stories, there is no protagonist, strictly speaking, although a few of the characters return in subsequent stories. The characters discussed here are especially notable for their relevance to themes of Cold War anxieties over war, political **totalitarianism**, and ecological devastation.

The Fourth Expedition

"June 2001: —And the Moon Be Still as Bright" tells of the

disastrous fourth expedition in which Spender attempts to kill his own crew, fearing that they will be the vanguard of a human invasion that will destroy the beauty of the now dead Martian culture. Several crew members from this mission appear later in the text as protagonists of their own adventures.

Spender

While Spender dies near the end of "—And the Moon Be Still as Bright," his warning to the crew of the fourth expedition— that humans will ruin Mars just as they ruined Earth— resonates many years later when Hathaway recalls the warning to Captain Wilder in "The Long Years":

> "Do you remember Spender, Captain?"
>
> "I've never forgotten him."
>
> "About once a year I walk up past his tomb. It looks like he got his way at last. He didn't want us to come here, and I suppose he's happy now that we've all gone away."

Spender is an archaeologist by training, and during his short time on Mars he quickly understands that the Martian civilization, which was wiped out by chicken pox brought by the first expeditions, had a deep and valuable culture. Spender believes that humans will compound the atrocity of unwittingly destroying the Martian species by thoughtlessly destroying the remnants of the culture and the planet itself. Spender tries to save the planet by killing members of his crew, but is ultimately fatally shot by Captain Wilder.

Captain Wilder

Captain Wilder leads the fourth expedition to Mars. Wilder sympathizes with Spender's point of view and attempts to reason with the crew members after the shooting. Following the difficulties of the expedition, Wilder is sent on long-term exploration to Jupiter, which is considered a demotion from his station on Mars. He reappears in the "The Long Years," where he returns from his exploratory missions to pick up the last survivors from Mars. There, Wilder and his crew find Hathaway—another fourth expedition crew member—living with his wife and children.

Hathaway

Although Hathaway's role in the fourth expedition is minor, he's a central figure in one of *The Martian Chronicles*' later stories, "The Long Years." Hathaway is marooned on Mars when the colonists return to Earth following the outbreak of nuclear war on the home planet. He and his family set up a simple, rural life in the hills. We later learn that Hathaway's family members have all died and are buried in a small graveyard near his house.

Captain Wilder and his crew find Hathaway when they return to Mars after many years. They soon discover that Hathaway has constructed lifelike and eternally youthful android versions of his deceased family. This is a sad reminder of the human desire for immortality and faith in technology to keep our memories alive. After Hathaway dies, his android family continues to live happily on Mars.

Sam Parkhill

One of the liveliest characters from the fourth expedition, Sam is especially incensed by Spender's treachery. After the expedition, he invests in a hot dog stand at a lonely crossroads he believes will soon be the site of heavy traffic. When war breaks out on Earth and the human population of Mars deserts the planet, the Martians who inhabit the land around the hot dog stand give him the property and flee the **scourge** of human invasion. Sam represents the human urge to selfishly succeed, and the human propensity to ignore the integrity of the environment or local traditions.

Americans Reacting to Change

William Stendahl

Stendahl is the protagonist of "Usher II," a story that departs in tone and content from the rest of the book but introduces ideas that are central to Bradbury's other works, in particular *Fahrenheit 451*, such as the scandal of destroying printed culture and the government's efforts to control its citizens by diminishing their capacity to think and read. Stendahl suffered censorship and loss of his precious library at the hands of the central authorities of a future American government bent on destroying literary imagination. He exacts revenge on these public officials by constructing an elaborate replica of the House of Usher from Edgar Allan Poe's famous short story and inviting them to a party in the house. Stendahl then orchestrates the guests' murders in accordance with various Poe stories. The murder of the government censorship official by confinement within a wall, for example, mimics the vengeful murder in Poe's "The Cask of Amontillado."

Walter Gripp

A comical version of the "last man" character, Walter Gripp (who appears in "The Silent Towns") was out of town when everyone left Mars upon hearing news of the war on Earth. He spends his days roaming the deserted towns. He hears a phone ring and eventually makes contact with a woman who was also left behind. He imagines she's beautiful, but she turns out to be repulsive and overbearing when he meets her. She indicates that since they are the only two people left on the planet that they should get married. Gripp immediately runs away in a desperate attempt to escape the horrifying woman. We learn from the crew members of the ship in "The Long Years" (who offer him a ride that he refuses) that Gripp doesn't want to return to Earth, preferring instead to spend his days alone on Mars. Gripp is a memorable if somewhat misogynistic comic interlude in an otherwise bleak portrayal of the failure of human progress.

Samuel Teece

Teece is a vengeful and bitter white Southerner who witnesses the mass exodus of the black population to rocket ships bound for Mars in "Way in the Middle of the Air." He is a caricature of Southern white bigotry, lording over black laborers and spending his free nights organizing lynch mobs. Through the action of the story, Teece becomes a symbol of callous individualism that contrasts against the compassionate collectivism of the departing black emigrants.

Major Themes

Aliens

Much of Bradbury's prolific output treats some version of the alien invasion narrative. Alien invasion narratives have long been popular in science fiction, especially since H.G. Wells' *The War of the Worlds* was published in 1898. It is useful to situate invasion stories from the Cold War era in the context of anxieties over Communism and fears of espionage.

Alien narratives can often be read as **xenophobic** or nationalistic fantasies. The alien figure may signify a foreign army, a foreign microbe, or a foreign species. When aliens appear, they are usually marked as different and threatening. Aliens come from other planets to wreak havoc on established human civilizations. With *The Martian Chronicles*, Bradbury has reversed this basic SF convention, making humans the invaders and Martians the victims of colonial expansion. Playing with this theme, Bradbury alludes to the history of North America. For example, the Martians are wiped out by chicken pox, reminding the reader of the smallpox epidemics that contributed to millions of deaths of Native Americans in the colonized New World. Bradbury's alien narrative is neither xenophobic nor nationalistic. Rather, *The Martian Chronicles* offers a critique of the United States as a new imperialist superpower, whose xenophobia and nationalism may lead it down a dark road.

Social Injustice

A number of stories in this collection take up issues of social injustice, both at the level of individual relationships and larger demographic forces. "Ylla" presents a portrait of the oppression of women in domestic spaces. It explores the problem of unequal gender relationships within social institutions such as marriage. On the other hand, "Way In the Middle of the Air" focuses on racial tensions in the South, and their connection to brute individualism. "—And the Moon Be Still as Bright" argues for a concept of justice that not only applies to families and races, but also civilizations and planets. Spender reminds us that, if we harm other people or the environment through our ignorance, it is our duty to keep ourselves out of ignorance. Every story of *The Martian Chronicles* remind us that adopting positions of gender, national, racial, or species supremacy leads to a world of suffering for all.

Love

The central emotional power of many of Bradbury's stories comes from their focus on love, which is often represented as lost or impossible. It is one of the peculiarities of SF that intensely human stories—of small-town childhood memories ("The Third Expedition") or the inability to accept the loss of one's family ("The Long Years"), for example—can be narrated within uncanny, alien settings. "Ylla" gains its power from a love that can only be realized in a dream, and "The Silent Towns," a comic inversion of a typical love story, depicts Walter Gripp's desperate desire to escape the shackles of romance. Bradbury uses the theme of love to give his stories emotional power.

In one sense, this is just good storytelling. But his meditations on love also relate to the cultural context of technology and humanism that motivated much science fiction at the time. In a world of machines, empty consumer culture, and fear, can we retain the love that we were born into as humans?

Illusion vs. Reality

As a setting, Mars is a kind of looking-glass world, a place in which it is never clear—to either the reader or Bradbury's characters—what is real and what is illusion. The deserts of Bradbury's Mars look like Earth, but they are red instead of brown. The air is breathable, but its thinness makes human visitors lightheaded. The small towns that the expeditionary teams encounter look like towns on Earth, but they are dangerous hallucinations. In "The Earth Men," the team wants to prove that they are from Earth, but the Martian ability to create hallucinations in others' minds is impossible to disprove—they are in a **Catch-22**. Bradbury's play with illusion and reality, insanity and sanity, calls into question the nature of our constructed realities, their inherent power to shape communities, and their dangerous tendency to blind us to truths worth knowing.

Major Symbols

Music

Although music is not central to the plots of these stories, there is a musical thread woven throughout *The Martian Chronicles*. Music symbolizes a variety of emotional and cultural truths. At the outset, music is an ominous presence: it appears telepathically in Martian daily life, infiltrating their dreams and festivals. In her dreams of the approaching human expedition, Ylla talks and sings with the astronaut Nathaniel York. In the following **vignette**, "The Summer Night," a riverside concert turns sinister when a Martian singer and her orchestra perform a song in English, presumably transmitted or received via telepathy. The lyrics are the opening **stanza** of Lord Byron's poem, "She Walks in Beauty Like the Night." The audience reacts viscerally to the "odd and ... frightening and ... strange song this woman sang." The foreign song confuses the singer and players because they don't understand the lyrics or the melody. The music they meant to enjoy, mutated by an outside force, becomes a warning: "And all around the nervous towns of Mars a similar thing had happened. A coldness had come, like white snow falling on the air."

In an inter-chapter entitled "Interim," we are given a glimpse of the newly colonized Mars, complete with replicas of small towns in America, where Bradbury remembers music was a welcoming presence and a conveyor of cultural meaning. Bradbury writes his own small town heritage into *The Martian Chronicles*, where hymns are sung in the Martian church on Sundays, and the sound of typewriters and pens (novelists and poets) can be heard from other houses. While the hymns of small-town America might evoke a pastoral calm in their original setting, they are intentionally weird and out of place on Mars.

Perhaps Bradbury's most striking use of music is as a symbol for the destruction of Martian culture in "The Musicians." In this very short story, young boys from the Mars colonies go gallivanting in the abandoned cities as a daredevil game, using the bones of dead Martians as xylophones and marimbas. Their game eventually ends when the Firemen (a precursor to the firemen in *Fahrenheit 451*) sweep through and destroy what is left of the Martian cities: "By the year's end, the Firemen had raked the autumn leaves and white xylophones away, and it was no more fun." Children often play a key role in Bradbury's fiction, and in this particular story, the juxtaposition of children's musical games with the genocide wrought by human invasion heightens the sense of horror the story evokes.

View of a row of houses in the kind of small, middle American town that inspired some of the stories in *The Martian Chronicles*.

The American Small Town

Bradbury, who was very much shaped by his origin in small-town Illinois, uses the middle-class American images of home and hearth in *The Martian Chronicles* to symbolize the inherent strangeness of "our own" way of life. For instance, the small town that the Third Expedition encounters looks suspiciously like the Captain's hometown of Green Bluff, Illinois, but is actually a hallucination meant to entrap and kill the crew. As the crew cautiously speculates about the town they're investigating, Hinkston the archaeologist asks, "Are we playing with something dangerous?" This story reinforces an idea that suffuses the entire book: At the heart of America and American virtue, even in small towns, is something dark, something that might lead to apocalyptic disasters like nuclear war.

Landscape

Much of *The Martian Chronicles* is devoted to illustrating dusty, rich, and twisted Martian landscapes. When Benjamin Driscoll (Bradbury's version of Johnny Appleseed) arrives on Mars, "the first thing he noticed was that there were no trees, no trees at all, as far as you could look in any direction. The land was down upon itself, a land of black loam, but nothing on it, not even grass. Air, he thought …" Driscoll and others see the desolate landscape and wonder how they can change it to suit their own ideas of what is right and useful.

While typical ideas of American progress demand that humans take charge of their environment and shape it to improve their lives, taking from the land can sometimes seem ugly. Spender reminds us that "there will be plenty of time … time to throw condensed-milk cans in the proud Martian canals; time for copies of the *New York Times* to blow and caper and rustle across the lone gray Martian sea bottoms; time for banana peels and picnic papers in the fluted, delicate ruins of the old Martian valley towns." What seems like a blank canvas for American progress can be perceived as ancient and pure, a natural state that progress, consumption, and industry is bound to destroy.

60TH ANNIVERSARY EDITION

FAHRENHEIT

451

RAY BRADBURY

With a new introduction by Neil Gaiman

at would I do, you mean, seriously?"

seriously."

n't know — I hadn't thought. She turned the handle of the silver

and placed the two cups in their saucers.

oured some coffee. In the background, the two small girls were pl

FOUR

Fahrenheit 451

Want the change. Be inspired by the flame
Where everything shines as it disappears.
—Rainer Maria Rilke, *Sonnets to Orpheus*, Part Two, XII

Writing and Publishing *Fahrenheit 451*

In a short essay entitled "Investing Dimes: *Fahrenheit 451*,"
Bradbury writes, "I didn't know it, but I was writing a dime
novel. In the spring of 1950 it cost me nine dollars and eighty
cents to write and finish the first draft of 'The Fire Man', which
later became *Fahrenheit 451*." To avoid being distracted by his
daughters at home, Bradbury sought the quiet of the University
of California, Los Angeles library. In the library's basement,
he discovered rows of typewriters at which he could work for
ten cents per half hour. When he wasn't working, Bradbury
walked among the stacks on the floors above. With the slightly
altered title, "The Fireman," Bradbury's story was published in a
magazine called *Galaxy Science Fiction* in February 1951.

Bradbury subsequently revised and expanded "The Fireman," incorporating an earlier short story called "The Pedestrian." After numerous unsuccessful attempts to find out from university science departments the temperature at which book paper combusts, Bradbury called the Los Angeles Fire Department, who informed him that book paper catches fire at 451 degrees Fahrenheit. (In reality, this is not necessarily true. Different kinds of paper, including different varieties of paper used for books, actually have different auto-ignition temperatures.) Bradbury's expanded story was published by Ballantine Books as *Fahrenheit 451* in a volume with two other stories, "And the Rock Cried Out" and "The Playground," in 1953. In an unusual move meant to reach the widest audience possible, Ballantine chose to release the book in hardcover and paperback editions simultaneously. *Fahrenheit 451* has since appeared without the other stories in numerous new editions, to which Bradbury has added introductions and a "Coda."

Events from Bradbury's Life that Shaped *Fahrenheit 451*

Bradbury was living in Los Angeles, California, when he wrote the stories that would later find their way into *Fahrenheit 451*. The idea for "The Pedestrian" came out of a specific incident in 1949, when Bradbury, walking late at night with a friend, was stopped and questioned by a policeman. Aware of his right to walk around his city whenever he wanted to, Bradbury responded sarcastically, "What am I *doing*? Just putting one foot in front of the other." Bradbury didn't appreciate the policeman's suspicion—they weren't doing anything wrong— and the policeman didn't like Bradbury's attitude.

This encounter and the ensuing argument prompted him to imagine a world in which walking is outlawed. Bradbury's concern was that if the right to walk in the street could be challenged by the authorities, other important rights could be

Bradbury and Censorship

In an ironic twist of events, Bradbury's novel was itself the victim of censorship from 1969 until 1979. An **expurgated** version of the novel was published in a Ballantine "Bal-Hi" student edition. This version removed references to drinking, drugs, and sex in order to make it acceptable to conservative school boards. The censored version inadvertently became the primary text used for reprinting the novel, and for six years the censored version of *Fahrenheit 451* was the only one in print. The error was discovered by students and eventually corrected.

This book refers to the unexpurgated sixtieth anniversary edition of the novel, published by Simon & Schuster in 2013.

called into question. "The Pedestrian" later became the opening scene of *Fahrenheit 451*, where Montag meets Clarisse McClellan while he's out for a walk. The rest of the narrative evolves out of this crucial encounter.

Plot Synopsis

Part 1: The Hearth and the Salamander

"The Hearth and the Salamander" opens with fireman Guy Montag returning from a night at work. In this future America, all of the houses are fireproof, so firemen no longer put out fires—instead, they start them. Books have been outlawed in this society, and firemen are responsible for enforcing their **prohibition**. They investigate suspected book owners and, if they find any books in their possession, the firemen burn the books and the book owners' houses.

Montag's views about his job, culture, and society begin to change after he meets Clarisse McClellan, a charming and peculiar seventeen-year-old girl who has moved in with her family next door. Clarisse is unlike anyone Montag has ever met before. Her thoughtfulness, inquisitiveness, and idiosyncrasies—she likes walking and conversation—make her stand out against the conformist society in which they live. During their initial meeting, Montag explains that he enjoys his job, and loves to smell the kerosene he sprays on the books to set them ablaze: "Kerosene," Montag tells Clarisse, "is nothing but perfume to me."

After this surprising and enjoyable conversation with Clarisse, Montag enters his home to find that his unhappy wife, Mildred, has overdosed on sleeping pills. He phones for help, and two indifferent men from the emergency hospital arrive soon afterward to revive her with a machine, saying, "We get these cases nine or ten a night. Got so many, starting a few years ago, we had the special machines built." When Montag confronts Mildred the next day, she's absorbed by her television program and refuses to acknowledge taking all of her sleeping pills the night before. Montag finally gives up and goes outside for a walk, where he meets Clarisse again. She tells him she loves to taste the rain. As Montag leaves her, he tilts his head back and lets the drops fall into his mouth.

At the firehouse that night, Montag senses that the Mechanical Hound—a killing machine used to hunt down book owners—might attack him. Montag wonders if the Hound is beginning to think for itself. Captain Beatty, the fire chief, explains, "It doesn't think anything we don't want to think." Beatty asks if Montag has a guilty conscious. A few days later, someone at the firehouse says, "Montag, a funny thing. Heard tell this morning. Fireman in Seattle, purposely set a Mechanical Hound to his own chemical complex and let it loose. What the hell kind of suicide would you call *that*?"

After a few conversations with Montag, Clarisse disappears without warning. When Mildred finally tells Montag that she was hit and killed by a car, he is appalled when he realizes that his wife knew of Clarisse's death four days before, but didn't bother to tell him until he asked.

Saddened by the loss of Clarisse, Montag becomes increasingly disillusioned with his profession. He learns that the person whose library they "fixed" recently was committed to an asylum, even though he wasn't insane. As Captain Beatty explains, "Any man's insane who thinks he can fool the government." When Montag asks if firemen once put out fires instead of starting them, one of his coworkers brings out the *Firemen of America Rulebook*, which contains this historical account:

Established, 1790, to burn English-influenced books in the Colonies.

First Fireman: Benjamin Franklin.

That night, the firemen go on a call to an old woman's house. Montag steals a book from her collection while his colleagues are distracted. The woman refuses to cooperate with the firemen, and defiantly lights herself on fire along with her books. Deeply disturbed by this incident, Montag later tells his wife, "[T]his fire'll last me the rest of my life. God! I've been trying to put it out, in my mind, all night."

Captain Beatty visits Montag at home to explain to him that books are outlawed because they are contradictory and encourage individuality in people. He relates the real history and rationale of the firemen. They destroy books because, ultimately, books make people unhappy: "We must all be alike. Not everyone born free and equal, but everyone *made* equal. Each man the image of every other; then all are happy ... So! A book is a loaded gun in the house next door. Burn it!" Beatty insists that the firemen protect the universal happiness that is their society's greatest achievement.

The chapter closes with Montag confessing to Mildred that he has accumulated a secret collection of books over the past year. Although Mildred is horrified, Montag is eager to find out what's so special about books that people are willing to risk their lives for them.

Part 2: The Sieve and the Sand

"The Sieve and the Sand" picks up with Montag and Mildred reading Montag's books. When Montag opens a book with the opening words, "That favorite subject, Myself," the narcissistic Mildred says, "I understand *that* one." Montag reflects that Clarisse's favorite subject was not herself, but other people. Unbeknownst to them, the Mechanical Hound sniffs around the Montags' door while they're reading.

Montag and Mildred hear the bombers flying overhead outside. Incensed, Montag asks, "How in hell did those bombers get up there every single second of our lives!"

The old woman and the firemen in a stage adaptation of *Fahrenheit 451*.
This performance took place at the Et Cetera Theatre in Moscow, Russia.

He suggests that the United States, after winning "two atomic wars since 2022," has become insular and **complacent**: "Is it because we're so rich and the rest of the world's so poor and we just don't care if they are?"

Montag remembers a man named Faber he once met in the park. Faber had been an English professor before books were banned, and Montag had kept his personal information in a file marked "FUTURE INVESTIGATIONS (?)" Montag goes to Faber's house to ask him about books. Faber is at first wary of Montag, but he relaxes when Montag shows

The futuristic "green bullet" radio communicator Bradbury imagined in *Fahrenheit 451* closely resembles the ear buds people use today.

him a copy of the Bible he brought with him. Faber tells Montag that books are feared in a totalitarian society like theirs because they "show the pores in the face of life. The comfortable people want only moon faces, poreless, hairless, expressionless." A book like the Bible "has *pores*," he explains to Montag. "This book can go under the microscope. You'll find life under the glass, streaming past in infinite profusion." In other words, books accentuate difference—infinite profusion—in the world, and difference is frightening and potentially subversive. Faber agrees to help Montag with his reading, and they concoct a risky scheme to overthrow the status quo. Before he leaves, Faber gives Montag a seashell-shaped radio transmitter he invented—the "green bullet"—to wear inside his ear so they can communicate.

At home, Mildred is entertaining guests. Fed up with the women's mindless chatter, Montag—despite Faber's warnings—brings out a book of poetry and begins reading Matthew Arnold's "Dover Beach" to them. Terrified and upset, the women leave in a hurry, while a furious Mildred locks herself in the bathroom. Montag leaves the house and talks to Faber through the transmitter in his ear while walking downtown. Faber reproaches him for the way he behaved towards the women, reminding Montag that he was just like them until recently.

When Montag arrives at the station house later that night, he notices that the Mechanical Hound isn't there. To avoid suspicion, he gives Beatty his Bible to burn. Beatty slyly rebukes Montag for his recent indiscretions: "That made you for a little while a drunkard. Read a few lines and off you go over the cliff. Bang, you're ready to blow up the world, chop off heads, knock down women and children, destroy authority." When the firemen go out on a call that night, Montag is shocked when they stop in front of his house.

Part 3: Burning Bright

"Burning Bright" opens with Beatty reprimanding Montag outside of the house. Mildred comes out with a suitcase, and Montag realizes she turned him in. She gets into a "beetle-taxi," crying, "poor family, poor family, oh everything gone, everything, everything gone now" as it drives away.

Beatty forces Montag to torch his home. Instead of using the kerosene pump and a lighter, Beatty prolongs the process by making Montag use a flamethrower. After Montag torches the house, Beatty explains that Mildred's friends turned him in before she did: "One way or the other, you'd have got it."

Through the transmitter, Faber begs Montag to run, but Montag's afraid the Mechanical Hound is out and programmed to track and kill him. When Beatty notices Montag tilting his head to listen, he knocks the green bullet out of his ear. Pocketing the device, Beatty threatens to trace it and "drop in on" Montag's friend. Turning the flamethrower on Beatty, Montag says, "We never burned *right*" before setting him ablaze. The Hound appears and briefly sinks its needle into Montag's leg, injecting him with a powerful anesthetic, before Montag destroys it with the flamethrower.

As Montag retrieves a few books that were hidden in his garden, he realizes that Beatty had wanted to die. With the anesthetic affecting his leg, he makes his way through the city to Faber's house. They watch the TV news and learn that Montag is wanted by the police, who are releasing another Mechanical Hound to find him. Faber tells Montag that he should head for St. Louis and see a retired printer who may be able to help them. To throw off the Hound, Faber gives Montag a suitcase packed with dirty laundry to mask Montag's scent. Faber promises he will follow behind on the first bus to St. Louis in the morning.

With the alarm raised across the city, Montag runs to the river and floats on his back for a long time, allowing the current to carry him along, before returning to shore. He walks through the wilderness and along a set of railroad tracks until he comes upon a group of people sitting around a fire. The group, called "the Book People," has been watching the chase on TV and recognize him. The leader of the group, a man named Granger, gives Montag a drink that will protect him from the Hound by altering the chemical composition of his sweat. Realizing that the authorities couldn't let it be known they'd lost track of the fugitive, the group watches the TV screen in horror as the Hound attacks an innocent man the police claim is Montag: "They didn't show the man's face in focus. Did you notice? Even your best friends couldn't tell if it was you."

Granger explains that the men in the group are all former professors. They, and thousands of others like them, live on the outskirts of society. They have developed a way to recall any book they've read: "All of us have photographic memories, but spend a lifetime learning how to block off things that are really *in* there." They are the repositories of the books they've read, and they invite Montag—who's read from the Book of Ecclesiastes and Revelations—to join their group. As they speak, atomic bombs fall and obliterate the city. The novel concludes with Montag and the men setting out for the destroyed city, determined to use the knowledge within them to rebuild civilization.

Cultural Context

Fahrenheit 451 is set in a future world that is in many ways not unlike our own. Bradbury envisioned the future so well that the novel's **prognostic** power often blinds readers to the fact that *Fahrenheit 451* is also very much of its own time. In the late 1940s and early 1950s, Senator Joseph McCarthy's and the House Un-American Activities Commission's persecution of people suspected of attempting to undermine American values was in full swing. Producers, writers, actors, and other major Hollywood figures were considered especially sympathetic to communism and were regularly targeted by McCarthyism.

Bradbury lived in Los Angeles at the time and was a member of the Screen Writers Guild. Many of his friends' and associates' civil liberties were under attack. Bradbury channeled his anger over the climate of intimidation, censorship, and oppression in Hollywood at the time into a short story called the "The Firemen," which would later be expanded into *Fahrenheit 451*. Captain Beatty's brute physical violence against an old woman book owner in the novel powerfully evokes the violence of certain United States government authorities against the Hollywood culture industry at the time.

The Hollywood Ten and the Blacklist

In 1947, ten Hollywood film industry figures–screenwriters and directors–spoke out against the House Un-American Activities Committee's investigation of communism's influence in Hollywood. They accused the committee of violating their civil rights. Known as the Hollywood Ten, they were arrested, fined $1,000 each, sentenced to one year in prison, and banned from working in the film industry. The Hollywood Ten became central figures in the controversy over the American House Un-American Committee's investigations.

In addition to the Hollywood Ten, other film actors, directors, screenwriters, and musicians who were accused of being communists or having communist sympathies were banned from working in Hollywood. Known as the Hollywood Blacklist, the ban was in effect from the late 1940s to 1960.

McCarthyism coincided with the Golden Age of Television, when TV had replaced radio as the major form of home entertainment—the era in which families first ate TV dinners on trays in their living rooms as they watched their favorite shows together. Television, which was sometimes called the "idiot box," provided such compelling and easy entertainment that many people thought it spelled the end of reading. Bradbury's novel reflects this anxiety in Mildred's inability to engage intelligently with the vapid programming she constantly watches: "What was it all about? Mildred couldn't say. Who was mad at whom? Mildred didn't quite know. What were they going to do? Well, said Mildred, wait around and see." Watching TV is largely a solitary activity, and for Mildred, TV hasn't merely replaced books—it's replaced other people. "'Now,' said Mildred, 'my "family" [that is, the people on TV] is people. They tell me things; I laugh, they laugh! And the colors!'" It is worthwhile to note that the fear that TV will "dumb us down," and that reading is losing ground to other forms of entertainment and learning, remains **prevalent** today.

In addition to the culture of fear surrounding communism and the prevalence of televisions in American households, Bradbury also addresses the nuclear proliferation of the time. It's important to remember that in 1945, a few years before Bradbury wrote *Fahrenheit 451*, the United States used nuclear weapons to destroy the Japanese cities of Hiroshima and Nagasaki, effectively ending World War II. It soon became clear that the United States wasn't the only nation to have effective nuclear weapons technology. The Cold War was on—and with it came widespread fear in the United States of imminent mutually assured destruction. In the world of *Fahrenheit 451*, the United States has already won two nuclear wars, and the next one is literally in the air. Ironically, most of the people in the novel's world are too narcissistically involved in their entertainment to pay much attention.

Major Characters

Guy Montag

Guy Montag is the protagonist of *Fahrenheit 451*. A fireman whose job is to burn books, he appears to enjoy his profession at the beginning of the novel: "It was a pleasure to see things eaten, blackened and *changed*." Montag's own change is initiated by a series of conversations he has with his neighbor, Clarisse McClellen, and the experience of witnessing an old woman allow herself to be burned rather than give up her books. These events ignite Montag's curiosity about the content of books. Montag eventually turns away from his job and his wife, and attempts to undermine the society that outlawed books and reading.

Mildred (Millie) Montag

Mildred Montag is Guy's wife. She watches mindless television programs—her "family"—all day on the large screens that make up three of the parlor walls. Although Mildred claims to not understand her husband's doubts about his job and the current political situation, she is far from happy. She barely survives an overdose on sleeping pills early in the novel. Mildred puts up with Montag's experiment with reading for a time, but turns on him—burning his stash of books and reporting him to the fire chief—after he insists on reading to a group of her friends.

Clarisse McClellan

Although Clarisse McClellen appears for only a few passages at the beginning of the novel, she profoundly affects Guy Montag. Clarisse is seventeen years old, beautiful, and describes herself as "crazy." She comes from an eccentric family that prefers to have conversation in the evening rather than watch the parlor walls. She's a close observer of the world around her, and soon sees that Montag is different from other people.

Clarisse disappears soon after meeting Montag. Mildred later reveals that Clarisse was killed by a speeding car.

Captain Beatty

Captain Beatty is chief of the firehouse at which Montag works. He's also an exceptionally well-read man with a deep knowledge of literature, rhetoric, and the history of ideas.
At first, Beatty tolerates Montag's curiosity about the books they burn. He explains the history of the firemen and tries to persuade Montag that books are confusing, contradictory, and worthless. After Mildred reports Montag to the authorities, Beatty forces Montag to burn his own house. Montag turns the kerosene hose on Beatty, and Beatty allows himself to be burned.

Professor Faber

Professor Faber is a former English professor. He lost his job when the liberal arts college where he taught closed. Montag goes to Faber to learn about books. Although Faber is initially reluctant even to speak with Montag, he agrees to talk Montag through his confrontations with Mildred and Captain Beatty using a small, seashell-shaped radio he invented that fits inside Montag's ear. A strong proponent of free thought and individuality, Faber encourages Montag to think for himself.

Granger

Granger is a member of the intellectual **diaspora** living on the outskirts of society. He helps Montag escape from the Mechanical Hound and invites him to join his group. Granger explains that there are thousands of people—"bums on the outside, libraries inside"—who have memorized books as a way to preserve them for future generations. They've developed a way to recall the books they've read even if they think they've forgotten them. Since they don't keep any physical books with them, they avoid harassment by the authorities.

The Old Woman

The old woman lives in a three-story house with an attic filled with books. The firemen investigate her house after a suspicious neighbor reports her. After the firemen douse her books with kerosene, she refuses to leave the house and uses a match to light her books, her house, and herself on fire. She appears only briefly in the novel, but her actions deeply trouble Montag: "There must be something in books, things we can't imagine, to make a woman stay in a burning house; there must be something there. You don't stay for nothing."

The Mechanical Hound

Instead of a live dog, the firehouse has a Mechanical Hound. The Hound has eight insect-like legs and a needle that it uses to inject its victims with a lethal dosage of anesthesia. The Hound is used to investigate and track down people suspected of possessing books. To pass the time, the firemen release rats, chickens, and cats for the Hound to track and kill. Montag believes someone has used his biological information—kept in a file in the firehouse—to program the Hound to dislike him.

Major Themes

Memory, Identity, and Community

In his introduction to *Modern Critical Interpretations: Ray Bradbury's Fahrenheit 451,* literary critic Harold Bloom writes, "I forgive the novel its stereotypes and its simplifications because of its prophetic hope that memory (and memorization!) is the answer." You can agree or disagree with Bloom's criticism of the novel's "stereotypes and simplifications"—although compelling arguments can be made for their inclusion in the novel—but his focus on memory is spot-on. Memory is crucial to forming a sense of identity and community. It provides a sense of continuity between who we've been and who we are, and allows us to envision who we might become in the future.

Early in the novel, Montag asks Mildred if she remembers when and where they first met. Unable to remember, she says, "Funny, how funny, not to remember where or when you met your husband or wife." She goes to the bathroom to swallow sleeping pills. For Montag, however, forgetting is far from funny: "He held both hands over his eyes and applied a steady pressure there as if to crush memory into place. It was suddenly more important than any other thing in a lifetime that he know where he had met Mildred." The future world of *Fahrenheit 451* is deeply invested in promoting self-centeredness in its inhabitants, which is not the same as fostering a strong sense of identity. Self-centeredness also weakens any possibility of real community.

The connection between memory, identity, and community is made explicit in the final pages of the novel. Granger tells Montag that the people who've memorized books form a larger community that, in the end, is more important than the individuals who make it up, explaining, "The most important single thing we had to pound into ourselves is that we were not important, we mustn't be pedants; we were not to feel superior to anyone else in the world. We're nothing more than dust jackets for books, of no significance otherwise." Although Granger's statements may seem extreme, the point is that the individuals who help ensure the preservation of the world's literary heritage are actually enormously important, but only in that they are part of something larger than themselves. In fact, *Fahrenheit 451* strongly suggests that without the world's great works of literature—in the largest sense of the term—and the stories they relate, the possibilities for forming strong communities of unique individuals is drastically reduced. The stories we tell literally make us who we are.

Nuclear War

The threat of nuclear war—"atomic war" in the text—hangs over the narrative of *Fahrenheit 451* like an ominous cloud. Montag explicitly calls attention to the constant presence of bombers in the sky, asking why no one is willing to discuss it.

Fahrenheit 451 imagines a future world in which libraries, like the New York Public Library shown here, have been outlawed and destroyed.

In the future world of the novel, the United States' nuclear power allows it to dominate and economically exploit the rest of the world: "I've heard rumors; the world is starving, but we're well fed. Is it true, the world works hard and we play?"

Although Bradbury's world is fictional, first-world military and economic dominance over third-world nations was and remains an undeniable reality.

The immense destructive potential of nuclear weapons is illustrated in the novel's final pages, which lend a menacing edge to the story's otherwise hopeful conclusion. After haunting every page of the novel, the war ends as soon as it's begun: "as quick as the whisper of a scythe the war was finished. Once the bomb release was yanked, it was over." The sense of imminent doom that hovers over the narrative and comes to a head in the novel's conclusion represent the fear of nuclear war that gripped the United States during the Cold War.

Major Symbol

Fire

Fahrenheit 451 opens famously with an evocation of fire's symbolic power as an agent of change, "It was a pleasure to burn. It was a pleasure to see things eaten, to see things blackened and changed." The remainder of the novel is devoted to Montag's struggle to change his identity from that of a fireman complacently fulfilling his function in society to a self-aware agent of his own destiny. Montag's transformation is ignited by his discussions with Clarisse, nourished by his revulsion at the burning of the old woman, and fulfilled by his wife's betrayal and his meeting with the "book people" in the wilderness outside of the city.

In addition to symbolizing change, fire symbolizes destruction. It not only destroys books, it also has the capacity to destroy people and cultures. As Captain Beatty tells Montag, fire is:

> "[P]erpetual motion; the thing man wanted to invent but never did. Or almost perpetual motion. If you'd let it go on, it'd burn our lifetimes out. What is fire?

It's a mystery ... Its real beauty is that it destroys responsibility and consequences. A problem gets too burdensome, then into the furnace with it. Now, Montag, you're a burden. And fire will lift you off my shoulders, clean, quick, sure; nothing to rot later."

However, as the novel's conclusion suggests, the destruction caused by fire—as long as it's not total—is a necessary condition of renewal. In the novel's final pages, Bradbury has the character of Granger invoke the ancient myth of the phoenix rising from the ashes:

"There was a silly damn bird called a Phoenix back before Christ, every few years he built a pyre and burned himself up. He must have been first cousin to Man. But every time he burnt himself up he sprang out of the ashes, he got himself born all over again. And it looks like we're doing the same thing, over and over, but we've got one thing the Phoenix never had. We know the damn silly thing we just did."

As Bradbury suggests, *Fahrenheit 451* is a warning, but it is also a reminder. It warns us about the possible mistakes of the future by reminding us of the mistakes of the past.

Timeline

1920 Ray Bradbury is born on August 22, in Waukegan, Illinois.

1926 Ray Bradbury's sister, Elizabeth Bradbury, is born. The Bradbury family moves to Tucson, Arizona.

1927 Elizabeth dies of pneumonia. The Bradbury family moves back to Waukegan.

1931 Bradbury begins writing stories.

1932 Family returns to Tucson. Ray Bradbury reads comic books to children on the radio.

1933 Family returns to Waukegan. Bradbury attends the World's Fair in Chicago with his aunt Neva.

1934 The Bradbury family moves to Los Angeles, California.

1937 Bradbury joins the Los Angeles Science Fiction League.

1938 Bradbury graduates from high school.

1939 Bradbury publishes a science fiction fanzine: *Futuria Fantasia*.

1941 Bradbury begins to support himself by writing full time.

1945 World War II ends with the United States dropping atomic bombs on the Japanese cities of Hiroshima and Nagasaki.

1947 Bradbury marries Marguerite McClure. He publishes *Dark Carnival*, his first book.

1949 Bradbury and Marguerite's first daughter, Susan, is born. The Soviet Union successfully tests first atomic bomb.

1950 *The Martian Chronicles* is published. The Korean War begins.

1951 *The Illustrated Man* is published. Bradbury and Marguerite's second daughter, Ramona, is born.

1952 Bradbury writes the story for the film *It Came from Outer Space*.

1953 *Fahrenheit 451* published. The Korean War ends.

1955 Bradbury and Marguerite's third daughter, Bettina, is born. The Warsaw Pact is formed.

1957 *Dandelion Wine* is published. Bradbury's father dies. The Soviets launch the first satellites into space.

1958 Bradbury and Marguerite's fourth daughter, Alexandra, is born.

Timeline

1961 The Berlin Wall is constructed by East Germany.

1962 The Cuban Missile Crisis threatens the world with nuclear war.

1965 The United States begins participation in the Vietnam War.

1966 Bradbury's mother dies. The film version of *Fahrenheit 451* is released.

1973 The United States withdraws its troops from Vietnam.

1977 Bradbury receives a Lifetime Achievement Award at the World Fantasy Convention.

1985 *Death is a Lonely Business* is published.

1989 The Berlin Wall is demolished.

1990 *A Graveyard for Lunatics* and *Zen in the Art of Writing* are published.

1991 The Warsaw Pact is dissolved and the Soviet Union is abolished.

2000 Bradbury is awarded the National Book Foundation's Medal for Distinguished Contribution to American Letters.

2002 Bradbury receives a star on the Hollywood Walk of Fame.

2003 Marguerite Bradbury dies on November 24, in Los Angeles, California.

2004 Bradbury wins the National Medal of Arts.

2007 Bradbury receives a special citation from the Pulitzer Prize for "his distinguished, prolific, and deeply influential career as an unmatched author of science fiction and fantasy."

2012 Ray Bradbury dies on June 5 in Los Angeles, California.

Bradbury's Most Important Works

Novels

The Martian Chronicles (1950)

Fahrenheit 451 (1953)

Dandelion Wine (1957)

Something Wicked This Way Comes (1962)

The Halloween Tree (1972)

Death is a Lonely Business (1985)

A Graveyard for Lunatics (1990)

Green Shadows, White Whale (1992)

From the Dust Returned (2001)

Let's All Kill Constance (2002)

Farewell Summer (2006)

Story Collections

Dark Carnival (1947)

The Illustrated Man (1951)

The Golden Apples of the Sun (1953)

The October Country (1955)

A Medicine for Melancholy (1959)

The Day it Rained Forever (1959)

The Small Assassin (1962)

R is for Rocket (1962)

Tomorrow Midnight (1966)

S is for Space (1966)

I Sing the Body Electric (1969)

Long After Midnight (1976)

The Fog Horn & Other Stories (1979)

Dinosaur Tales (1983)

A Memory of Murder (1984)

The Toynbee Convector (1988)

The Parrot Who Met Papa (1991)

Quicker Than The Eye (1996)

Driving Blind (1997)

The Playground (2001)

One More for the Road (2002)

Is That You, Herb? (2003)

The Cat's Pajamas: Stories (2004)

A Sound of Thunder and Other Stories (2005)

The Dragon Who Ate His Tail (2007)

Now and Forever: Somewhere a Band is Playing and Leviathan '99 (2007)

Summer Morning, Summer Night (2007)

We'll Always Have Paris: Stories (2009)

A Pleasure to Burn (2010)

Individual Stories of Note

"The Scythe" (1943)

"The Million Year Picnic" (1946)

"The Small Assassin" (1947)

Bradbury's Most Important Works

"Fever Dream" (1948)

"The Long Years" (1948)

"Dark They Were, and Golden-Eyed" (1949)

"The Veldt" (1950)

"There Will Come Soft Rains" (1950)

"Ylla" (1950)

"The Fog Horn" (1951)

"The Fireman" (1951)

"A Sound of Thunder" (1952)

"The Wilderness" (1952)

"All Summer in a Day" (1954)

"The Best of All Possible Worlds" (1960)

"The Mummies of Guanajuato" (1978)

"The Aqueduct" (1979)

"The Toynbee Convector"(1984)

"From the Dust Returned" (1994)

"Is That You, Herb?" (2003)

Glossary

android
A robot that looks or acts like a human being.

antagonist
Opposite of "protagonist," the character who is in direct conflict with the protagonist. "Antagonists" are two people or groups in conflict with one another.

aqueous
Made of or containing water or liquid, water-like.

callous
Unfeeling, insensitive to other's emotions, cruel or mean.

canonical
Part of a small group of extremely important examples, usually a group of books or authors.

Catch-22
An inescapable dilemma that is the result of paradoxical or contradictory rules, from the novel *Catch-22* by Joseph Heller.

celestial
Heavenly, having to do with the heavens or outer space.

complacent
An attitude of lazy contentment with what one has achieved.

containment
The policy outlined by the U.S. whose purpose was to keep Soviet and Chinese Communism contained within their own borders.

coup
Short for *coup d'état*, from the French meaning "stroke of state," a sudden and often violent overthrow of a government or leader.

Glossary

diaspora
A group of people living outside the area in which they had lived for a long time or in which their ancestors lived.

doctrine
An official foreign policy or program, often used to name major U.S. foreign policies.

dystopian
Opposite of "utopian," a type of story that imagines a dark, sinister, or otherwise bad future, often involving totalitarian governments and the loss of personal freedoms.

epitomize
To be a perfect example of something.

eponymous
A person or character's name that is given to a title; for example, the character Ylla gives her name to the story "Ylla."

expurgated
Edited to remove parts considered offensive or inappropriate.

innumerable
Countless, very many.

juxtaposition
The placement of two objects or qualities next to one another for comparison or contrast.

lurid
Shocking, vivid, or sensational, often used to describe bright or harsh colors.

nuclear winter
The theoretical period of darkness and cold after a nuclear war caused by the massive clouds of dust that would be kicked up by the explosions.

ostensive
Showing what it means to show, demonstrates clearly.

prevalent
Common, widespread.

prognostic
Predicting an outcome or future, sometimes used to describe a doctor's prediction of the outcome of a disease (prognosis).

prohibition
A rule that forbids or makes something illegal.

proliferation
A rapid increase in quantity, often used to describe the increase in nuclear stockpiles.

protagonist
The main character of a story, usually the character whose point of view dominates the narrative.

proxy wars
Wars fought between opponents who are not necessarily on the battlefield. For example, the Soviets support the North Koreans in battle, while the United States supports the South Koreans.

redolent
Strongly reminiscent of something; also, sweet smelling.

Glossary

rhetoric
The use of speech or written language to persuade, artful argumentation.

scourge
Something that is the cause of great calamity or disaster.

stanza
A group of lines in a poem that form recurring "verses."

totalitarianism
A form of government, rule by a dictator or strong centralized governing body with "total" power.

veneer
A thin outer shell, figuratively meaning the shallow appearance of something rather than its true essence.

vignette
A short episodic story or brief account of some activity.

xenophobic
Fear of outsiders or foreigners, often taking on the characteristics of racism.

Sources

Introduction

Pp. 5–6: Atwood, Margaret. *In Other Worlds* (New York, NY: Anchor, 2011), p. 6.

P. 7: Mogen, David. *Ray Bradbury*, (Boston, MA: Twayne, 1986), p. 83.

P. 7: Bradbury, Ray. *Fahrenheit 451* (New York, NY: Simon & Schuster, 2013), p. 151.

Chapter 2

P. 29: Nolan, William F. *The Ray Bradbury Companion* (Detroit, MI: Gale Research, 1975), p. 5.

P. 31: Winorski, Jim, Ed. *They Came from Outer Space* (New York, NY: Doubleday, 1981), p. xi.

P. 31: de Koster, Katie, Ed. *Readings on Fahrenheit 451*, p. 17.

P. 32: Wallace, David Foster. "ZDF Interview, 2003: On Education." http://www.youtube.com/watch?v=N5IDAnB_rns

P. 34: "A Century of Progress." Chicagohs.org. 1999. Web. 17 March 2014. http://www.chicagohs.org/history/century.html

P. 35: de Koster, Katie, Ed. *Readings on Fahrenheit 451*, p. 20.

Pp. 36–37: de Koster, Katie, Ed. *Readings on Fahrenheit 451*, p. 21.

P. 37: Johnson, Wayne L. *Ray Bradbury*, p. 4.

Sources

P. 39: Bradbury, Ray. "National Book Awards Acceptance Speech." (National Book Foundation).

P. 41: de Koster, Katie, Ed. *Readings on Fahrenheit 451*, p. 28.

P. 42: de Koster, Katie, Ed. *Readings on Fahrenheit 451*, p. 28.

Chapter 3

All quotations from *The Martian Chronicles* are from the 2012 Simon & Schuster edition.

Chapter 4

P. 71: Ray Bradbury. "Investing Dimes: Fahrenheit 451." *Fahrenheit 451*. Ed. Jonathan R. Eller (New York: Simon & Schuster), p. 199.

P. 72: Eller, Jonathan R. "The Story of Fahrenheit 451." *Fahrenheit 451*, p. 172.

All quotations from *Fahrenheit 451* are from the 2013 Simon & Schuster edition.

Further Information

Books

Eller. Jonathan R. *Becoming Ray Bradbury*. Urbana, IL: University of Illinois Press, 2013.

Harrison, Paul. *Why Did The Cold War Happen?* (Moments in History). New York, NY: Gareth Stevens, 2010.

Leiva, Steven Paul. *Searching for Ray Bradbury: Writings About the Writer and the Man*. Pasadena, CA: Blüroof, 2013.

Sewel, Mike. *The Cold War* (Cambridge Perspectives on History). Cambridge, England: Cambridge University Press, 2002.

Weller, Sam. *Listen to the Echoes: The Ray Bradbury Interviews*. Brooklyn, NY: Melville House, 2010.

Websites

The Official Ray Bradbury Website
www.raybradbury.com

The official website of Ray Bradbury contains a brief biography and chronology of the writer, a bibliography of his works, and useful links to articles, book reviews, and interviews.

Further Information

Science Fiction & Fantasy Writers of America

www.sfwa.org

Science Fiction & Fantasy Writers of America is an organization for authors of SF and other related genres. The SFWA website contains a wealth of information, including information on the prestigious Nebula Awards for the year's best novel, novella, novelette, short story, and script.

Science Fiction Site

www.sfsite.com

Science Fiction Site contains a ton of information for SF fans, including book reviews, interviews with authors, and useful reading lists.

Cold War

www.history.com/topics/cold-war

History.com provides a multimedia approach to Cold War history. The site is organized by topics (the Cuban Missile Crisis, U-2 Spy Incident, Ronald Reagan, to name a few), each of which contains textual, audio, and video resources and a photo gallery.

Bibliography

Atwood. Margaret. *In Other Worlds: SF and the Human Imagination*. New York, NY: Anchor, 2011.

Barrass, Gordon S. *The Great Cold War: A Journey Through the Hall of Mirrors*. Stanford, CA: Stanford Security Studies/Stanford University Press, 2009.

Belletto, Steven, and Daniel Grausam. *American Literature and Culture in an Age of Cold War: A Critical Reassessment*. Iowa City, IA: University of Iowa, 2012.

Bloom, Harold, Ed. *Modern Critical Interpretations: Ray Bradbury's Fahrenheit 451*. Philadelphia, PA: Chelsea House, 2001.

—. *Ray Bradbury*. Philadelphia, PA: Chelsea House, 2001.

Bradbury, Ray. *Fahrenheit 451*. Edited by Jonathan R. Eller. New York, NY: Simon & Schuster, 2013.

—. "Investing Dimes: Fahrenheit 451." *Fahrenheit 451*. Edited by Jonathan R. Eller. New York, NY: Simon & Schuster, 2013, pp. 199-208.

—. *The Martian Chronicles*. New York, NY: Simon & Schuster, 2012.

—. "National Book Awards Acceptance Speech." National Book Foundation. Retrieved February 3, 2014 from www.nationalbook.org

Bibliography

Chicago History Museum. "A Century of Progress." Retrieved February 12, 2014 from www.chicagohs.org

Crossley, Robert. *Imagining Mars: A Literary History.* Middletown, CT: Wesleyan University Press, 2011.

de Koster, Katie, Ed. *Readings on Fahrenheit 451.* San Diego, CA: Greenhaven, 2000.

Eller, Jonathan R. "The Story of Fahrenheit 451." Ray Bradbury. *Fahrenheit 451.* Edited by Jonathan R. Eller. New York, NY: Simon & Schuster, 2013, pp. 167-188.

Gaddis, John Lewis. *The Cold War: A New History.* New York, NY: Penguin, 2005.

Hammond, Andrew. *Cold War Literature: Writing the Global Conflict.* London, England: Routledge, 2006.

Hoffman, David E. *The Dead Hand: The Untold Story of the Cold War Arms Race and Its Dangerous Legacy.* New York, NY: Anchor, 2010.

Inskeep, Steve. "Interview: Ray Bradbury Discusses NASA's Current Mars Mission And President Bush's Vision For Space Exploration." Weekend All Things Considered (NPR): Newspaper Source Plus.

Johnson, Wayne L. *Ray Bradbury.* New York, NY: Ungar, 1980.

Judge, Edward H., and John W. Langdon. *The Cold War: A Global History with Documents.* Boston, MA: Prentice Hall, 2011.

McMahon, Robert J. *The Cold War: A Very Short Introduction*. Oxford, England: Oxford University Press, 2003.

Mogen, David. *Ray Bradbury*. Boston, MA: Twayne, 1986.

Nolan, William F. *The Ray Bradbury Companion*. Detroit, MI: Gale Research, 1975, p. 5.

Reid, Robin Anne. *Ray Bradbury: A Critical Companion*. Westport, CT: Greenwood, 2000.

Rubin, Andrew. *Archives of Authority: Empire, Culture, and the Cold War*. Princeton, NJ: Princeton University Press, 2012.

Wallace, David Foster. "ZDF Interview, 2003: On Education." YouTube. YouTube, July 15, 2010. Retrieved March 17, 2014 from https://www.youtube.com/watch?v=q78j9WmvoKo

Walker, Martin. *The Cold War: A History*. New York, NY: H. Holt, 1995.

Weller, Sam. "Marguerite Bradbury: 1922-2003." Retrieved February 12, 2014 from www.raybradbury.com.

Winorski, Jim, Ed. *They Came from Outer Space: 12 Classic Science Fiction Tales that Became Major Motion Pictures*. New York, NY: Doubleday, 1981.

Index

About the Authors

Joseph Kampff holds a Master's degree in English and an advanced graduate certificate in Cultural Studies from Stony Brook University. He's interested in representations of trauma and violence in the contemporary global novel.

Greg Clinton is a PhD candidate in Cultural Studies at SUNY Stony Brook. His research focuses on infection and contagion in literature and film, as well as the politics and philosophy of literature and ecology. He has taught both literature and philosophy at the high school and undergraduate levels. Greg has lived in the United States, Egypt, Belgium, Japan, Sudan, and India.